One Lesbian's Journey to Her Resurrected Identity

COMING OUT
WITH

KAROL ADAMS
Foreword by Brian Phipps

To Emma—

You are truly God's wonderful gift
of life and love

To the LGBTQ Community—

God has always loved you

To the One True Messiah—
(Yeshua—Jesus)

You are my Rock, my Refuge,
and my First Love

Karol has courageously shared her story in a way that will validate and liberate others through the power of a resurrected identity in Christ. This book is authentic and prophetic, comforting and challenging. Please do yourself a favor and join Karol as she shares her journey; you will find yourself closer to Jesus and better equipped to walk with others who are on this path.

Rob Wegner
Leader, Kansas City Underground; co-author, *Find Your Place*

Karol Adams is the real deal! With transparency and authenticity, Karol shares a powerful story of a love that captures hearts and lovingly but stubbornly compels those who hear it to surrender to the grace and mercy that can only find in a personal relationship with God. I couldn't put the book down once I started! It is simply the powerful story of one woman's relentless search for God. Despite unbelievable obstacles, pits, and pain, Karol never gave up. And the result is a life that shouts, "God loves me and will pursue me to the ends of the earth!"
From empty to full
From darkness to light
From bondage to freedom
From broken into beautiful
From death into life
Karol is faithfully living out God's plan for her life as she staunchly shares her journey with other seekers—including members of the LGBTQ community. But Karol has taken it a step farther. She has not only boldly shared her story, but she has become a living illustration of God's love as she has shown others how to find the freedom she has found. It is my honor to wholeheartedly endorse this book!

Mary Southerland
Author, speaker, member of Girlfriends in God

Karol's story is an important one. She's not some ivory-tower philosopher, academically hypothesizing about the ins and outs of life in the LGBTQ community. She knows firsthand what it's like. She's been there. She understands. She's lived it. More importantly, she knows life on the other side: redeemed by Jesus, reconciled to her Heavenly Father. Her experience is not theoretical; it's real life. And that matters. My wife and I met Karol at just the right time. She became a guide for us, walking with us as we sought to understand the life some of our friends and family members were living. Under her tutelage, we gained empathy and understanding as well as a firm understanding of the Bible's unwavering stance on these issues. As you'll discover

upon reading this book, our friend Karol is as humble and honest as she is helpful and hopeful. Karol is gracious and gospel-centered. Above all, Karol loves Jesus and loves you, too.
Barrett Case
Pastor, Rich Hill Christian Church

Often the conversation of identity focuses on who I am and what I do, or even who I sleep with or am attracted to. One's true identity, however, has very little to do with all of that. Instead, getting to the heart of your true identity is about surrendering what you believe about yourself in order to encounter the fullness of Christ in your life. That is the heart of Karol's book, *Coming Out with Christ.* Karol's personal identity story challenges today's cultural narrative on this subject with humility, honesty, and hope. *Coming Out with Christ* is a must-read for anyone who has wrestled with judgment, shame, or confusion about their identity—which I personally believe is all of us.
Crystal Renaud Day, MAPC
Founder, Living on Purpose & SheRecovery.com
Author, *90 Days to Wholeness* & *Dating Done Right*

Karol tells a compelling story. And like every story of God's redemptive love, it is deeply personal and unique in nature. Each of us, whoever we are and wherever we have come from, will glean insights and inspiration from *Coming Out with Christ.*
Deb Hirsch, Missional Leader and Speaker
Author, *Redeeming Sex; Naked Conversations about Sexuality and Spirituality*

Foreword

We all need heroes.

Heroes are people we admire for their courage, outstanding achievements, and noble qualities. We need heroes to inspire a similar courage in us. The world becomes a better place as more and more people courageously step into the highest calling any life can fulfill: the calling to love God and love others with a sacrificial love.

I believe Karol Adams is this kind of hero.

Karol has demonstrated exceptional boldness and courage by simply putting her story in writing. By doing so, she is voluntarily entering into a politically-charged arena with nothing more than her vulnerable self and honest story. If history is any indicator, both she and her story will be misunderstood and misrepresented by strong and often violently opposing voices. The politically conservative voice will undoubtedly challenge her for her observations about her early life. With similar earnest, the politically liberal voice will challenge her transformed views and behaviors regarding sexuality starting around the birth of her daughter. Karol could easily keep this story to herself and live at peace…at least from the outside.

But heroes fear internal turmoil more than external.

Potential heroes get leveled down to living normal lives when external threats squelch their internal calling. Karol has refused to do that. She has been told to speak. Jesus Himself has asked Karol to share her story as an invitation for everyone, conservative and liberal alike, to see two things: first, how much Jesus loves people; second how radically transformational Jesus' love can be. Like the prophets of old, Karol must share what God has given her to share. I am grateful for her courage to do so.

I believe Karol's courage is an inevitable product of the outstanding achievements God has accomplished through her so far. She has tirelessly shared her story with members of the LGBTQ community. More than this, she has served the loved ones of those LGBTQ members who were hurt, confused, and even alienated by these choices. Her story has helped many of those relationships find healing. Understanding and grace have been offered. Spiritual transformation has occurred. Karol has been asked to speak on many occasions, sharing her story with large numbers of adults and teens at conferences, retreats, and groups. To extend this impact, she has established her own 501c3 ministry called SOIL. These outstanding achievements are simply the result of her obedience to Jesus' leadership in her life; this book is simply the next step.

Jesus is the epitome of noble qualities and character. Jesus, through His Spirit, empowers His followers to cultivate that same character in their lives. Karol is a notable example of that transformation. She is a woman marked by a unique blend of grace and poise. This was the first thing I noticed about Karol when we first met. She was not angry toward me, even though she expected me to be less than kind to her due to the fact that I am a pastor. She was not posturing with a false sense of strength to prove herself to me. Her life was simply what it was…a story being written by the masterful hand of Jesus. Though filled with grace, she is not weak. She is strong, intelligent, and articulate. Karol's strength comes from a very deep place…a lifetime of challenges posed by her own painful experiences blended with God's persistent pursuit and love for her in the midst of those challenges. This blend of grace and strength is what Jesus calls "meekness". Jesus says the meek with inherit the earth. I trust that this meekness will at least merit your benefit of the doubt.

I hope two things for you as you read Karol's story.

First, I hope her story increases your compassion for anyone struggling with any kind of sexual and gender confusion. Every human is made in the image of God and therefore is deserving of being treated with dignity. Every human is fighting a great battle, and every one of those humans needs grace and understanding to win in that battle. Regardless of a person's struggle, those are our people to love.

Second, I hope you do more than simply see the changes in Karol's life. I hope her life causes you to truly long for the catalytic transformation that Jesus, through the Holy Spirit, can bring to your life, regardless of the battle you are fighting. Karol is a walking miracle, formed and fashioned through a million steps of faithful obedience. Karol's path is unique to her, but the pattern of her path is the same for everyone: Jesus changes our lives by first changing our identity.

Allow Karol's courage to inspire courage in you. Allow her achievements to be examples of what God can do through your obedient life. Allow her character to be a model for how you live your life. For in doing so, you can become a hero yourself.

Enjoy Karol's story.

Brian Phipps, founder of Disciples Made, co-author of *Find Your Place*

Acknowledgements

I am so grateful to the team of women writers who carried me, from start to finish, through this monumental project. Without Molly, Bridget, Pam, Kim, Jenny, Britta, and my daughter Emma, I would have failed. Because of their invested time, talents, and faithful support, I was able to finish the task that God had placed on my heart nearly three years ago. I believe they each were brought to me at the right place at the right time to fulfill a divine purpose that will be beyond all imagination.

I am so grateful for Dave, Phuc, Jen, and the other Christians I met early on, who helped me find my way back into the Church. God used each of them through their generous acts of kindness, goodness, and acceptance to help me find where I belong in God's House.

I am eternally grateful for Breanna, Deni, Shirley, Jeannie, Aileen, Michelle, Tamara, Kelley, Bobbi, Nicole, and Laura, my eleven Disciples Made women, who wholeheartedly embraced me as one of their own. Through each woman's personality and spiritual giftedness, they taught me valuable wisdom and gave me new confidence as a genuine woman of God and a true sister in Christ. They will always be the chosen apostles that first loved me and showed me what it meant to be a real disciple of Jesus.

I am grateful for the disciple-making leaders surrounding me. I am thankful for Brian Phipps and his vision for Disciples Made. With big faith and courage, Brian continues to follow after Jesus' heart and mission. I am also grateful for the leaders of Kansas City Underground. KC Underground is built on the DNA of the early church and founded by the movement of the Holy Spirit for prophetic times, such as now. Because of these leaders' faith and obedience, Jesus is awakening a new era of reproducing disciples to their passion, purpose, and calling…to finish what Jesus started.

Lastly, I am tremendously grateful for all of the prayer warriors who have prayed tirelessly for me and my daughter throughout our lives, and for the mission of Step Out in Love (SOIL) Ministries. "The smoke of the incense, *together with the prayers of God's people*, went up before God from the angel's hand" (Revelation 8:4, emphasis added by author). I believe God hears and answers the prayers of his righteous ones, so please, keep praying.

Table of Contents

INTRODUCTION

Normal. That is how I would have described myself at age eleven. Nothing about me stood out from the crowd, except maybe my quirky sense of humor and my tomboy mannerisms. I felt like an ordinary kid.

Summer started out as usual, except this particular one turned into a life-altering season. That was the summer I met Emily. She was a newcomer to my mother and stepfather's circle of friends. For whatever reason, this thirty-something divorcee caught my attention. Upon our encounter, I was struck by her beauty, as well as her gentle and nurturing soul.

Because of her attentive nature, Emily offered sweet terms of endearment along with individual attention. I figured Emily could sense my insecurities and emotional cravings. Regardless of her intentions, her affection unleashed internal havoc. My mind stirred with these charged and intoxicating feelings that I could neither explain nor resist. Everything about this woman awakened me to an emotional thirst I refused to deny. Although I could not consciously identify those strange feelings then, I know now that I was experiencing my first same-sex crush.

After our first encounter, I could not stop myself from daydreaming about Emily. I was obsessed with everything about her: her gentle voice; her long, wavy hair; and her beautiful green eyes. My feelings toward Emily felt exhilarating and fulfilling, which led me to believe they were healthy. I thought, how could something so real, unique, and satisfying be wrong? I was so confident in my feelings that I openly and willingly expressed how I felt toward Emily to everyone, including her. I wrote her letters, spilling out my genuine feelings for her and my ongoing desire to be around her. At this point, I had no thought or reason to hide or be afraid of this unique friendship. I innocently believed that my feelings for Emily were completely natural. I felt no shame.

In late July, my middle sister and I were once again visiting our biological mother, stepfather, and our oldest sister, and I could not wait to see Emily again.

Late one afternoon, while napping on the couch in my mother's living room, I awoke to sounds of escalated voices coming from the adjoining kitchen. The intense conversation immediately drew me in as I heard them mention my name. I kept still while I eavesdropped on the conversation. I nearly stopped breathing so I could listen to every word.

My mother was instigating the roundtable discussion, and her captive audience was my two sisters. This was an intense and intimidating family debate that soon identified me as the person of interest. The tone of their voices was making me extremely uneasy. I was getting the feeling that something was horribly wrong. My mind started racing through my most recent actions, wondering what I had done to draw such scrutiny.

Then came the context. The focus was on my peculiar behavior with Emily. Although I could detect the sizzling judgment and condemnation, my naïve mind could not imagine the implications. What was wrong with how I felt toward Emily?

Then came the defining moment when my mother blurted, "I am disgusted with Karol and how she acts around Emily. It is not right, I tell you!" A split second later, these cutting words came from the same mouth, "She's a freak!!!" The old saying, *sticks and stones may break my bones, but words will never hurt me,* is a big fat lie. My mother's words impaled me.

I laid there for a few seconds, frozen in fear and confusion, wishing I could snap my fingers and disappear in thin air. At that moment, my life forever changed. For the first time, I felt horrifying shame.

To feel guilt or conviction, there would have to be a feeling of wrongdoing. I was clueless about what I was doing wrong, but that did not matter. No one was asking me to explain. No one was asking me about anything. That brought me to the conclusion that it was either too sick or too perverted to discuss. Since there was something wrong with my feelings and behavior, then there had to be something horribly wrong with me. How could I possibly separate the two?

Like a typical child's reaction to fear and shame, I pretended nothing had ever happened. I buried this incident as deep in my mind as it would go.

As for Emily, I never saw her again. She dropped out of my life as quickly as she stepped in. I emotionally withdrew from my family. I abruptly stopped sharing all my thoughts and feelings about women with anyone. To sustain acceptance, approval, and a shred of normalcy, I kept all my thoughts and feelings as near to me as a betting hand of poker.

I believe most, if not every, same-sex-attracted people experience an eerily similar defining incident such as this. A catalytic, pivotal moment when they forever lose their innocence and hope for healthy and natural sexuality. A moment when fear, doubt, and shame attempt to kill, steal, and destroy their identity…and an instance when they try to adapt to the world's truth for their truth.

We are compelled to sell out everything just to find something. It was at this exact moment when my journey to finding my resurrected identity began.

Victory

They triumphed over Satan by the blood of the Lamb
and by the word of their testimony.

Revelation 12:11a

PART I

A SELF-MADE IDENTITY

1

GENESIS

Children are not things to be molded but are people to be unfolded.
Jess Lair

A Given Name

Every new life is given a name. I believe every name has a significant meaning and purpose. Names given to our children often represent family traditions, personal preferences, prosperity, and popularity...or for some, a spiritual destiny.

Although my parents were expecting their third child to be a boy, by chance or destiny they were given another girl. They had already picked out their boy names, and since my gender was a surprise, they had to quickly come up with a girl's name. They chose one of the more popular first names of the decade and gave it a slight twist. They named me Karol, spelled with a K instead of a C. It certainly gives my name pizzazz and uniqueness. My nickname became *Karol with a K*.

In some cultures, the name *Karol* means 'masculine' and 'manly'. In other societies, it means 'song of joy'. Thus, I could say that the name Karol means I am destined to be a joyful, masculine woman. I certainly do believe our given names reveal our identity and orient us toward our purpose in life...our destiny.

Shaky Foundation

Six years before I was born, my parents conceived their first child out of wedlock. Both were young, my mother only fifteen years of age and my father twenty-three. In those days, the proper thing to do was to get married before the illegitimate child was born.

After eight years of marriage and three daughters, my parents were divorced just months after they celebrated my first birthday. My mother had gone from a fifteen-year-old student to a stay-at-home mother and housewife to a twenty-three-year-old single mother of three small children under the age of seven.

Mom and Dad's personal choices and decisions led to equally accountable and substantial consequences. The most substantial penalty fell upon my mother. The judicial system granted our mother full custody of all three children with the expectation of our father paying alimony and child support. My father did neither. Placing sole responsibility of raising three small children onto a young, uneducated mother in the late '60s was doomed to fail.

During the brief time we lived alone with our mother, my eldest sister, Rachel, adopted my sister and me. As our surrogate mother, she felt responsible for dressing, feeding, and caring for us even though she was only seven years old. I latched onto Rachel as if she were my natural mother.

In a matter of only weeks to months, our mother fell to anxiety and depression. It was at this point of no return when she reluctantly abandoned and surrendered her three children. Tiffany and I, at ages five and two, were the first to be separated from her. Since Rachel was older and could care for herself, she stayed with our mother a few months longer before she too was separated from her. Less than two years after my parents' divorce, all three of us lost contact with our biological mother.

As a self-employed, long-distance, long-haul truck owner and driver, my father was not really capable of managing three children on his own. It was just a matter of time before both parents resigned and delegated their parental rights and responsibilities to others. Our parents divided the three of us and placed us into different homes. It was their makeshift plan while they attempted to piece together their broken lives.

Tiffany and I were left with my dad's youngest brother, J.W., his wife, Marilyn, and their family. J.W. and Marilyn introduced us to our cousins, Demi, who was twelve, and Dawson, who was seven. J.W. and Marilyn's family instantly grew from a family of four to six.

Rachel, who was now nine and the one I was most dependent on and attached to, moved in with another uncle's family. Letting go of Rachel was as difficult as letting go of my parents. Before turning three, I was drowning in various depths of emotional and physical abandonment.

Longing for stability, I swiftly adjusted to my new makeshift family. Since J.W. worked as a farm tenant for a local farmer, he and his family lived out near the western edge of Missouri's rural countryside. Every window of the farmhouse had panoramic views of rolling pastures and cultivated fields. Our closest neighbors lived miles away rather than blocks away. I took to country living like a child to sweets: I had plenty of open pastures and fields to run and explore, horses to ride, dogs and cats to raise, and other children to play with. J.W.'s place soon became my safe haven.

Yet, there was more than just the country living that won me over. I quickly cultivated bonds and attachments to every member of my makeshift family—my other family.

Uncle J.W. soon ranked as a childhood hero. J.W. loved children, and he offered his time and affection to Tiffany and me like we were his own. It was not long before I loved and adored Uncle J.W. like a father. I truly worshipped both of my gods, J.W. and my dad. Like children often do, I could only see the good, not the bad, in these two men.

No doubt, Marilyn was the backbone of this family. Although she was not the official head of the household, Marilyn earned the title. She did it all. Until I had to start kindergarten, I was Marilyn's daily sidekick. I often followed her around while she tucked and tidied the house. I was also her sole travel companion when she made weekly trips to the local laundromat and supermarkets. I sometimes got a box of animal crackers all to myself to preoccupy me while Marilyn shopped. Not having to share treats with the three other siblings made me feel special. It was in these unique moments that I capitalized on Marilyn's attention. Trying to gain Marilyn's approval was my ongoing plight. I instinctively knew my livelihood depended upon these relationships. Even at this early age, I was operating in survivor's mode, working every angle of every situation just to earn and secure a rightful place in the family.

Because Demi was only a bit older than Rachel, I quickly attached myself to Demi. Although she was not my sister by birth, I chose her by heart. I soon nicknamed Demi as my "cheater" sister. It was a creative term of endearment determined by a three-year-old who wholeheartedly missed her older biological sister. Demi was also my protector. In our four-way sibling rivalries, she consistently came to my defense. Demi's nurturing presence helped fill the emotional void created from the absence of Rachel.

Dawson was all boy and acted like a typical, tormenting big brother. He, too, became my protector. I knew he would stand by me, no matter what.

Tiffany was my much-needed refuge and emotional anchor. Her presence alone gave me a sense of stability and security. Tiffany was my comrade who knew and shared the same pain and anguish I felt from the loss of our father, mother, and oldest sister. She was my best friend and playmate. I seldom shared my deepest feelings, but if I did, I shared them with Tiffany. We played together, protected one another, and got on each other's nerves. Even though I could never admit it, Tiffany was the childhood rock that helped me endure many storms—environmentally and emotionally.

Every member of this makeshift family soon became a tethered lifeline for this rescued orphan.

Family Remnant

Remnants of my biological family were salvaged. Tiffany and I continued to have a relationship with Rachel and our father. Our acquired families supported and encouraged us to have an ongoing connection and relationship with our dad.

Dad was chained financially and emotionally to his long-haul trucking business. Even though all of his daughters were transitioned into his brothers' families, he never gave up his authority or title as Dad. He was a proud father, and, despite the fact he was a part-time father, all three of us were his number one fans.

Although Dad, Rachel, Tiffany, and I lived only approximately twenty-five miles apart, we were only able to visit as a family during special occasions and planned getaways. Some of my greatest childhood memories were made during my adventures with our father. It was not the destination that mattered most but the privilege of being reunited with my innate family.

Even though I was only four years old, I can still remember bits and pieces of our first family adventure. Dad piled our suitcases and the three of us into his car, and we headed West. He drove us to see the Grand Canyon while visiting one of his elder sisters who lived nearby. Then he took us to Yellowstone National Park in Montana. It was a long drive, so one night we slept in his car. Dad was either thrifty or broke because we seldom stayed in hotels. Because I was shortest and smallest, my overnight spot was on the narrow shelf of the car's backseat window. I remember lying on my back and staring at the limitless stars twinkling across the horizon of the western night skies. It was in these few and fleeting moments that I could let go and let my life's challenges and worries fade away into the heavens above. Each of these times gave me a momentary sense of feeling like I belonged.

Once we arrived at Yellowstone, Dad let each of us feed marshmallows by hand to large, hungry grizzly bears through partially rolled down car windows. Dad was a bit of a rebel who usually disregarded all safety rules and guidelines, which, from a kid's perspective, made him even more thrilling and exciting to be around.

The trips I treasured most were the times we traveled with Dad in his big semitruck. I loved to smell the burning diesel and to pull the bighorn chain as people passed us. My designated riding spot was standing on the "doghouse" (the built-in engine compartment). I could stand up and still have inches of head clearance from the top of the truck's cabin. One of the ways he kept us entertained on these long routes was singing. He loved country and western music, and he taught us to sing his favorite songs. At night, the three of us slept together in the cab sleeper while Dad slept in the back of the semitrailer, which was usually loaded with fresh onions. My afternoon naps often happened while sleep-standing on the doghouse, holding tightly to the strapped handle just outside the cab sleeper. I never wanted to sleep alone in the cab sleeper for fear of waking up and finding myself left behind. The thought of losing my father like I lost my mother had become my scariest nightmare.

The hardest concept for me as a child was understanding why our trips had to end. In the last hours together, the giggles and singing stopped and melancholy moved in. When we would pull into the driveway of Uncle J.W.'s farmhouse, tears would begin to stream down my face. I had to let go of my daddy all over again. I did not understand why I had to live apart from him. What I wanted was the same rightful privilege that Demi and Dawson took for granted: to live with my father and mother. My most suppressed feeling was fearing my dad might never come back for me again. He would simply vanish. The threat was real, and because of it, I never wanted to leave my daddy's side.

Even as a part-time family, we were still able to make lasting memories. That made a difference in my sense of well-being. What kept me hopeful was believing that someday my remaining biological family would once again be reunited. I was counting on Dad to make this dream come true.

Gender Confusion

Fear of abandonment was one of my worst childhood enemies. The other was my gender identity. I was a little girl who subconsciously wanted to be a boy. These inner feelings of not wanting to be a girl surfaced years before I could understand or explain them. Between the ages of three and four, I repeatedly displayed warning signs of dissatisfaction and discontentment with my gender identity as a girl. Before I could articulate full sentences, I was vehemently rejecting toys, clothes, and roles that associated me with being a girl, and innocently gravitating toward the identity of a boy.

The first circumstantial evidence of my confusion with my gender identity was in how I wanted to express my gender. What I wanted to wear and what I was expected to wear were direct opposites. Back then, girls always wore dresses and the boys wore pants with pockets. In our first couple of years living with J.W. and Marilyn, Aunt Marilyn often dressed Tiffany and me in matching dresses. I hated wearing dresses because dresses made me look like a girl. My favorite childhood outfit consisted of a boy-like shirt, pants, cowboy hat, and cowboy boots. My cowboy boots were essential attire because both my dad and Uncle J.W. always wore cowboy boots. I wanted to wear nothing except what identified me as my heroes and my cousin, Dawson.

Another hidden expression of gender confusion was in my hair. Aunt Marilyn washed and curled all the girls' hair every single day. Once she snapped those soft, spongy, pink curlers in place, I could barely wiggle my tiny fingers between the curlers and my scalp. Sometimes she rolled the strands of hair so tight, it would bring tears to my eyes. I hated this daily ritual so much that when she was finished, I would escape to a hiding place, then sit and cry. Once I stopped crying, I would try to sabotage the curlers, hoping they would fall out prematurely. My long, curly locks of hair were a sickening reminder that I was a girl. I continuously wanted my hair to look like Dawson and J.W.'s haircuts, which were very short and shaved above the ears. Hair length and styles were a stereotypical expression of what boys and girls were supposed to look like. It was one gender expression I could control.

My make-believe role-playing was another giveaway to my heart's desire. I never wanted to pretend to be a wife or a mother. I ultimately rejected all models, roles, and activities, along with appearances, that were associated with women, especially a mother. My fairy-tale fantasies always identified me as the prince on the white horse, rescuing and marrying the princess. I always wanted to be the husband or the father, or I refused to play. These roles gave me permission to be what I desired to be.

Other stereotypical high-water marks were toys and activities. I rejected dolls, dollhouses, and girly toys. Instead, I wanted all the coolest toys Dawson owned, like guns, army soldiers, cars and trucks, sports equipment, etc. Once, Uncle J.W. brought home this large doll. It was practically as tall as me. When they surprised me with it, I gave a scouring look, threw down the baby doll, crossed my arms, and began to cry. Needless to say, J.W. and Marilyn stopped buying me dolls and started buying more gender-neutral gifts like books, games, and guitars. My experiences with gender-based toys were the early signs that revealed my intense inner dislike of being a girl and a strong desire to be a boy.

My chosen role models were another indicator of gender confusion. Which parental role I decided to identify with and which one I rejected was significant. I clearly identified with the alpha men in my life: Dad and Uncle J.W. It is a healthy and reasonable expectation for little girls to idolize their fathers and want to be Daddy's little girl. In fact, it is known for girls to grow up and choose their future husbands based on the characteristics and personality of their fathers. However, that was not me. I had no fantasies or desires to marry men who were like my father or uncle. Instead, I wanted to be a husband like my paternal heroes and have a wife. I did not fantasize about being a wife; rather, I fantasized about having a wife.

There was more evidence in the stereotypical activities I chose to engage in and avoid because of how they were associated with gender. I resented the chores and activities that linked me with the expectant duties and responsibilities of women. I hated cooking, cleaning, dishes, laundry, etc. They were all monotonous feminine duties and responsibilities that kept me locked indoors. This was an era where men's perspectives and opinions on the value and purpose of women were quite siloed. Women were here on earth for one thing: to have and raise babies and keep the house in order. Men were the leaders and providers of the family. I hated and resented this whole ideology. I was adamant and determined to be the provider, not the homemaker. Because of my strong feelings and desires to be manly, I not only detached myself and my identity from the maternal roles but also the women who filled them. Ironically, I saw these women as weaker and lesser than men.

In this remote and rural region during the late '60s, words like gender confusion, gender identity, or gender expression were never spoken at schools, around the dinner table, or even in the hottest neighborhood gossip rings. Back then, I had no understanding of what I was feeling or why I was feeling it. My developing brain could not discern, comprehend, or communicate such confusing and complicated feelings of gender confusion. Nor did anyone in my family have a clue. Because of this, the warning signs of gender confusion flew under everyone's radar.

A Child's Identity

The first six years of life left a significant imprint on my identity. Psychologists call this stage of early childhood development the formative years. It is from birth to the first few years of a child's life when they learn to define themselves and form their identity of whom they think they are. My character was unfolding.

Despite the fact I was rescued and placed in a caring, stable, and fostering home, the impact of my formative years was undeniable and irreversible. The evidence clearly shows that the foundation of my identity as a child was cracked, exposed, and vulnerable. I continuously wrestled with a sense of security, belonging, and who I was. I was never confident in knowing where I belonged and whom I belonged to. My family picture felt like a temporary image. The paint never dried on the canvas, and the scene could easily smudge. From day to day, week to week, and month to month, the people I attached myself to and the places I stayed were under constant threat of changing or becoming another disappearing act. Poof, and it could all vanish. Nothing felt permanent.

2

RAISED BY A VILLAGE

Children crave to feel needed, valued, and recognized as a part of the family. To a child, belonging means to feel noticed, included, accepted, and loved.
Richard O'Keef, How to Get Kids to Behave

Five years went by, and our makeshift family transitioned into our primitive family. I identified myself as a rightful member of Marilyn's side of the family, as well as a native from the Adams family. Tiffany and I were embraced by Marilyn's biological family. Marilyn's two brothers and one sister became aunts and uncles, and their children were my favorite cousins. I admired everyone in Marilyn's family, but the two I cherished most were Marilyn's mother and father. They treated me like their own grandchild, and I called them Grandpa and Grandma.

While growing up, I spent many nights and days with Grandpa and Grandma. When life felt boring or chaotic, I went to Grandpa. Being around him made me feel like everything would be okay.

We shared the love of farming. Where Grandpa went, I went, and we usually spent hours and hours tinkering around the farm. He soon became my wise counsel and best friend. In some ways, Grandpa and I were at a time in our lives where we needed each other. He was growing older and weaker due to his troubling heart disease, and I needed someone to notice me. Grandpa gave me special attention, but, more importantly, he believed in me. He too was my hero, and a hero can make all the difference in the world.

Maternal Reunion

Every child instinctively knows where they come from—one father and one mother. This biological factor is clearly known even in the animal kingdom. Children do not have to look far to find and identify what family is and what it should look like. If a child's family looks and feels different than the norm, they want to know why.

Time could not erase the fact that Tiffany and I were without our biological mother. Tiffany was old enough to remember bits and pieces of our mother and remembering made it even harder for her to understand why our mother had abandoned her. I, on the other hand, could not remember anything about our mother. Because of our age difference, our ways of searching for answers varied drastically, yet the impact was the same. We had no one to call Mommy.

Tiffany had come to her own conclusion about our mother. Since our mother had never returned for her, she must have died. There was no other logical explanation. Without memories, I questioned her existence entirely. If she did exist, where was she? Why did she not come back for me, or want me? After months, then years, passed, I stopped asking why and Tiffany stopped waiting.

Resigning ourselves to the fact we were motherless, Tiffany and I proposed our own solution to our dilemma. We wanted to address Aunt Marilyn as "Mom". Understandably, this infringed on Demi and Dawson's rights, and our idea was denied. The rejection was based on two technicalities. This was supposed to be a makeshift plan. I believe everyone was hoping that one of our biological parents would return and resume full responsibility for raising their children. The second technicality was that we were not their biological children, so the inheritance did not belong to us. Even though Marilyn was as close to a mother as one could get, we obeyed and continued to identify Marilyn as our aunt and nothing else.

During my eighth year of life and my fifth year of living with Uncle J.W. and Aunt Marilyn, my world was rocked. Midmorning, Marilyn called Tiffany and me downstairs to the family room. My first thought was, "uh-oh, we are in trouble!" As I dreadfully stepped off the last stairstep onto the carpeted floor of our living room, my attention was quickly diverted to a visiting stranger. While keeping my eyes fixated on this unidentified woman, I quietly sat down on the couch. Marilyn then said, "Come, say hello to your mother." Her words echoed in my head like a shouting voice in the Grand Canyon. I could not believe my eyes. After wondering for nearly six years, I was sitting face to face with my real mother.

My stomach churned like I was preparing to jump out of an airplane at 10,000 feet in the air. Could this strange woman be my mother? I carefully examined this foreigner from head to toe. She was modeling this fancy, blonde, beehive hairdo that was several inches higher than the top of her head. Her face was full of life with her bright brownish-green eyes and a smile. Then out of her mouth came this low and raspy voice inviting me to come to sit by her. After seeking Marilyn's nonverbal approval, I went and sat on my mother's lap. At the age of eight, I was meeting my mother. I was in a whirlwind of emotions, having a hard time sorting through and processing all my thoughts, doubts, and feelings.

My mother was finally at a place in her life where she was ready to step back into our lives. From her perspective, I can only imagine how hard it would be to face your children after being absent from their lives for so long. My mother had come with good intentions. She had remarried, and together they were ready to start their own family.

Tiffany and I learned that Rachel had already left her makeshift family and had moved in with our mother and stepfather. She was thirteen, which granted her the right to decide for herself where she wanted to live. I was still clinging to the hope of my biological family being reunited through my father, not my estranged mother. I did not know what to think or feel.

Despite our mother's intentions, things did not go as planned. Our mother and stepfather challenged our biological father for custody of Tiffany and me, yet the judicial system ruled and implemented a different strategy. Due to both of our parents failing to meet the minimum parental requirements according to family law and practice, the court appointed Uncle J.W. and Aunt Marilyn as our legal guardians. There was no doubt that the court made the right decision. Uprooting us from the people who had raised us and from the comfortable home we had lived in for the past six years would have made a detrimental impact on our well-being.

My family identity was now confirmed.

Family Triage

My family turned into a village. From age eight to eighteen, I tried to navigate and triage my affection, devotion, and loyalty among three diverse families. My upbringing revolved around my legal guardians, J.W. and Marilyn; my biological father; and the latest contenders, my biological mother and stepfather. It was an emotional balancing act and tug-of-war between these three entities.

I was not necessarily compliant with my mother's maternal reinstatement. I was the least forgiving person toward my mother, and I made it known. Forgiveness was unimaginable. In my heart and mind, there was no plausible explanation for abandoning her daughters...and for six years. I could not find one shred of credible evidence that proved my mother was innocent. At the pound of the gavel, I sentenced my mother with reckless neglect and abandonment. Regrettably, my resentment and hatred imprisoned me and shut the door on reconciliation.

I did grow to love and respect my stepfather, but at arm's length. He was a kind, caring, and good-hearted man who earned the family title and nickname of Poppy. He was also a loyal and faithful husband to our mother, but to a fault. His loyalty spoiled our mother like a king treats his queen, and because of it, she got whatever she wanted. Although Poppy was a good guy, he was still my mother's ally, and that made him my enemy.

There was one attraction that compelled me to stay in contact with my mother: Rachel. Every visit to see my mother presented opportunities to rekindle our sisterhood. Being with Rachel and Tiffany was always an exhilarating and fun-packed experience. Rachel was, indeed, a free spirit. I admired her self-confidence, beauty, and boldness to pursue whatever she wanted. In some ways, Rachel and I were a carbon copy of each other. Even though I was tall and skinny and she was short and curvy, we shared like minds. We were both left-handed and could eerily fill in each other's jokes, thoughts, and actions. There was one significant difference between us. She was a rule breaker, and I was a rule follower. She never worried or feared life's consequences, while I worried about and feared every aspect of life. Our likes and differences always kept me drawn to Rachel.

Having our mother reenter center stage created a whole new dramatic scene with our biological father. Our father never got over losing our mother, and, though it was a dysfunctional and destructive marriage, he never stopped loving her. Eventually, though, he too moved on. Dad met a divorced woman who was raising her two sons on her own. Interestingly, her two sons were near the same ages as Tiffany and me. Dad's world extended to his girlfriend, his three biological daughters, and two newly acquired sons.

The fact that my dad was living with this woman and raising her two sons infuriated me. These two boys were living in my rightful place with my dad. The whole situation hurt like salt on an open wound. Why would my dad choose to raise these two boys and not me? I envied and resented this family because they had what I desperately wanted: a daily relationship with my father. My father was my dad, not theirs.

Resentment ran deep on the other side, too. These two boys resented and despised our father as their new authoritative figure. It was apparent that Dad favored his daughters over them. His favoritism was a rub on these boys' abandoned hearts from their own father. It was clearly a broken and dysfunctional mess.

It was far from easy for me to adapt and balance my identity between three extraordinarily diverse families. I struggled psychologically as I tried to express my devotion and loyalty across the lines between the natural and the adopted. Trying to find self-worth, acceptance, and belonging in one family was hard enough. Trying to find it among three families felt impossible. Loving one family without offending or abandoning another was like strategically walking through a land mine. One misstep or misspoken word would set off an explosion. I did not want to risk or jeopardize one family to gain another. I relied heavily on performance and compliant behavior to sustain acceptance and approval from all three sides. That was not always enough to mitigate the constant rivalry and jealousy across territorial lines. My mother hated my father and resented his side of the family, while J.W. and Marilyn felt disrespected and betrayed whenever we sided with our biological parents. I fiercely hated being trapped in the parental crossfires.

Found Faith

It was through our regular attendance in church that I learned about God and faith. Every Sunday morning, Marilyn woke up four sleepy kids, dressed us in our best clothes, and took us to church. Although J.W. rarely went with us, we seldom missed church.

I do not ever recall questioning the existence of God. He has always been real.

Church was a different story. Going to church was my least favorite thing to do. I did not want to be among crowds of people, and I strongly disliked the mandatory dress code. My other dislike was Sunday school. In my class, I felt like an uneducated misfit. Most of my peers where proteges of their parents' faith and obedience. These children knew everything about the Bible and could quote Scripture like a recording. As for me, I did not own a Bible, and, even if I did, I really did not want to read it. I hated reading as much as I hated dresses. Like J.W., going to church was really not my thing.

The church was not where I saw God. I first found God through His earthly creation. When things got chaotic or troubling, I took to the outdoors. I spent hours and hours being outside alone because this was where I could always find peace. Being outdoors took my mind off the seriousness of life and into exploratory missions. There seemed to be endless places for a curious kid to find in the remote and rural countryside. Every expedition started with a party of three—my imagination, my dog, and God. On these footed journeys, I talked endlessly to my faithful and loyal companions. Both were good listeners that gave me a safe place to escape.

Seldom did God speak to me. However, I believed wholeheartedly that He heard me and was getting a daily list of my worries and concerns. There was a particular instance where God unexpectedly answered one of my cries. One afternoon, I got into an argument with Dawson and Tiffany. I cannot recall what exactly we were fighting about, but I do remember storming off in anger and tears.

I really needed someone to hear me and my side of the story, so I went to God. The matter was so important to discuss that I had to meet God where I thought He lived. So, I took out my bicycle and peddled down a dusty gravel road about a mile away to the tiny, single-room building called Bethel Church.

After reaching the building, I hopped off my bike and tried opening the front double-sided doors, but they were locked. I was still determined to reach God, so the front steps of the church had to do. I kneeled on the concrete steps, then bowed my head and prayed aloud. I told God about everything Dawson and Tiffany did and said to me, then I boldly asked Him to punish them. As soon as I said amen, I felt as light as a feather. In place of anger, God gave me overwhelming peace and joy. God heard and immediately answered my prayer, although it was not exactly what I had asked for.

I hopped back on my bike and strolled home in song and laughter. I was singing because God had heard me and taken away my burden. Of course, He did not release His wrath on Tiffany and Dawson, as I had hoped for. Instead, God gave me something much better than vengeance: His love and attention.

Family Identity

Is it possible for a child to be raised by a village of people and still feel unwanted or misplaced? Unfortunately, yes. I am not at all placing all the blame on the villagers or their environments. I equally place weight and emphasis on the child's cognitive thinking and perception of their feelings and experiences.

My childlike comprehension of my surrounding families and experiences was this: people fought hard over me, but not for me. I believe my mother and father's internal and external battles were fought more out of a need to save themselves than to keep their children. That was, and still is, a prevalent story among broken families. Until the cycle is broken, history repeats itself. While my parents' domestic fights raged on, their children remained prisoners of war. J.W. and Marilyn rescued us out of pity, obligation, and good conscience, but not because they wanted more children.

My childhood perception, which may have some truth, left me believing I was not genuinely desired, valued, or recognized as an unconditionally loved and wanted child. I was made part of a family by appointment, not choice. And when it comes to a child having a sense of belonging, feeling chosen is at the core of their family identity.

3

SELF-DISCOVERY

If being gay is a choice,
then when did you decide to become straight?
Human Equality

Gender Dissatisfaction

No one can escape sexuality. It is an inevitable, developmental phase of humanity that everyone experiences at one point or another. However, the truth is, not all of us experience it in the same way. The journey of figuring out my sexuality was not as 'straight'-forward as I had expected or hoped for.

While my height sprouted up like Jack's beanstalk, my womanhood seemed to have stalled out. My female peers gracefully transformed from awkward ducklings into swans, yet my physique remained unchanged. I had no bust, waistline curves, or hips. I inherited the infamous nickname, "String Bean". I did look like a freshly picked, green, garden string bean—long, straight, and skinny. Yet, I was okay with my tomboy body because my heart's desire was to be a boy.

The conflict between my secret desire to be a man versus a woman went on. I continued to secretively fantasize about my desired gender—being a boy and becoming a man. My delay in womanhood only gave me false hope that I might actually be a boy trapped in a girl's body. My reality and illusion were about to have a head-on collision.

My body was undeniably, though slowly, becoming a woman, and I hated every second of it. Watching the physiological changes turn me from a girl into a young woman brought anxiety and depression. The effects of adolescence were killing off my dreams and fantasies. Although I never hated my body image, what I felt on the inside about my gender identity grossly misaligned to what I saw on the outside.

There were other indirect harbored feelings of gender dysphoria that I never wanted to confess. I coveted Dawson's identity. He was a handsome, intelligent, and charming young man that drew the attention of many women, and we seemed to have similar tastes. I had a girl-crush on a few of the women Dawson dated. His break-ups became my imaginary break-ups. Besides getting all the girls, Dawson was also a privileged boy. He was born as J.W.'s legendary only son, and, in his rightful position, Dawson inherited special favors with authoritative privileges. I resented the paternal pecking order in our household. Men invariably were first before women. Dawson was freely given everything I longed for.

Alongside my adolescent changes, my early-childhood gender confusion transitioned into open-ended gender discontentment and dissatisfaction.

Am I a Lesbian?

If a person looks or acts differently than their peers, that person can become a target for bullying. I soon became a target for two apparent reasons: lacking a woman's mature body and little to no sexual desire for boys. I was quickly pegged.

The first target was my tomboyish physique. The running joke was, I had a "tit-less" shot rather than a tetanus shot. That was humiliating. Then came the heckling and harassment from boys for not putting out. Rumors were floating around about my lackluster sexual attention and participation with the opposite sex. There was one obnoxious young man that kept publicly teasing me by saying I did not like boys because I was a lesbian. Then he would follow up with an obscene gesture of licking his tongue in between his index and middle finger. What did that even mean? It could not be right, or he would not tease me about it. What gave him the idea that I was a lesbian? What could he see that I could not see? I was in the dark, and, as always, that frightened me. Maybe he was attracted to me, and this was his way of dealing with rejection? Not likely, though. Whatever his motives were, the bullying and teasing finally got under my skin.

When someone calls us something, we always want to know what they mean, whether it is positive or negative. I was curious about this new hippy-like terminology—lesbian. Before I could defend myself and deny the accusations, I had to find out what this word meant. I could not strategically fight back if I did not know what I was fighting against. Knowing this guy's reputation, the term had to be sexually charged and, most likely, immoral. That was all I had to go on.

I grabbed the dictionary from our bookshelves and hid in the most secluded place in our house—our basement. Then I began to thumb through the words until I reached the letter *L*. As I perused the words in order, I could feel my heart beating rapidly against my chest while my hands trembled like a leaf in the wind.

The Webster Dictionary's definition read something like this: "Lesbian: A woman who is a homosexual." It was the word *homosexual* that sent chills up my spine. It was such a cold and clinical word with no empathy or feeling attached. Is that what I was? I reread the definition again and again.

As I sat there alone, thoughts and feelings came rushing in like opened floodgates. I was beginning to connect the dots. I remembered the painful incident during the summer before my twelfth birthday when my own mother questioned me because of my feelings and emotional attraction toward Emily. Now, between the ages of twelve and fifteen, I was suspiciously challenged and targeted as being a lesbian. The allegations and labels came well before the perceived abominable act. Even though I was innocent, when my eyes focused on the word lesbian, I saw its associated synonym—*freak*.

The dictionary had a definition but no further advice or instructions. I needed others to help me navigate these feelings and determine what I should do about them. Turning them off was impossible. Without having anyone I felt I could turn to, I took matters into my own hands—I chose to deny, hide, and compartmentalize my real feelings. Out of protection, I let people see only what I wanted them to see. The rest of me remained hidden.

To shield myself from further criticism and scrutiny, I needed to quickly camouflage my true colors. To blend in, I had to look and act like them. That meant I needed a credible heterosexual identity. This strategy was going to cost me integrity, but that was a sacrifice I had to make to protect myself, my innocence, and my reputation.

My livelihood depended on the acceptance and approval of my peers, friends, and family. I had already wrestled with my sense of belonging and citizenship among family—and now this? I felt I had no choice but to lie. Although I profoundly hated liars that lied to make themselves look good or always be right, this lie was paramount to my protection. The cost of exposing myself could cost me everything. One thing my childhood taught me was that abandonment meant rejection. This self-discovery of forbidden sexuality could cost me everything I had left, including my village. Although my family was complicated, I still needed them. I frantically worried about these rumors drifting back to my family. That left me with only one option: fake my heterosexuality and lie about my evolving homosexuality.

Talk can only go so far. I knew the walk had to follow the straight talk, and this meant I had to engage, to some degree, in heterosexual behavior. Maybe my heterosexuality was late, like my femininity. I was doubtful, though.

I tagged a few guys as boyfriends, per se, and did a little heterosexual experimenting. Even though these guys were sweet and attractive, I never felt any emotional connections or a burning sexual desire to be with them. When it came to men, nothing sparked, and because of it, I felt like I was going through the motions.

This falsehood became a juggling act. While trying to sustain a steady boyfriend, I had to continuously pretend I liked boys around all the other girls. Every girl near my age was crazy about boys, except me. All of this made me feel like an exiled foreigner in my own backyard.

To fill in the void, I poured my energy into my academics and athletics, especially basketball. Basketball was my go-to sport. Since third grade, I had aspired to play high school and collegiate basketball. It was the sport I loved most, and it paid out the highest dividends in terms of accolades and rewards. Knowing that J.W. and Marilyn were proud of my academic and athletic performances, I strived even harder. My academic and athletic achievements brought much-needed affirmation and personal attention from family, friends, and fans, and it was a welcomed diversion from my sexuality challenges.

As I quietly witnessed my peers flourish and recklessly indulge in their awakened sexuality, I questioned if I would ever find mine. There was little to no hope of finding everlasting love and happiness. There was little to no dream of someday having my own family. If I did, could I ever share my true self with others without facing hatred, judgment, and condemnation? Again, I was filled with doubt.

Introduction to Christianity

One afternoon, I was surprised to see our church's preacher come to our home. It was his first and last visit. I was even more surprised that the reason for his visit concerned me. Amid all my other fluctuating adolescent changes, our preacher popped a very personal question. Was I ready to be baptized?

I understood the intent and seriousness of the preacher's question, but not the real meaning and purpose of baptism. I thought that if I did not take this next step, I would be sacrificing the hope in eternal life and forfeiting my Christianity. Who consciously chooses to go to hell?

Opposite of my discovered sexuality, this was a choice. At age thirteen, I made an oath before God and plunged into Christianity as I understood it. It was a marvelous and unforgettable spiritual experience. As the preacher pulled me up out of the water, my heart and body felt as light as a feather. Momentarily, I felt clean, shameless, and joyful before God.

I was now a Christian with all my sin washed away. What sin then was washed clean? The typical teenage temptations were pre-marital sex, drugs, alcohol, cigarette smoking...more importantly, were my feelings toward women a sin or a temptation? Were temptations a sin? At this young age, I could not answer these questions. What I could answer, though, was my accounted sin for such things as lying to avoid severe consequences, cheating on tests, smoking cigarettes, drinking alcohol as a minor, and committing one petty theft. None of these sins owned me. I could only decipher sin with its associated guilt. Even though others may have perceived me as a perverted or lost sinner, I felt no remorse or guilt for my same-sex feelings. However, I did feel a deep sense of remorse and guilt for lying and hiding the truth. Lies were my most substantial burden.

Hidden Identity

"Who am I?" That was my question. As a young adult, I was pretending to be what I thought I was supposed to be—a heterosexual Christian. After feeling like a misfit and an outcast as a child, the last thing I wanted was for my sexuality to further alienate and exile me from others.

Throughout my adolescent years, I silently battled with my gender identity and sexual identity. I was keeping so many dark secrets hidden from everyone because of the festering, deep-seated fears of rejection and abandonment. A critic's words of judgment and condemnation were hard to stomach, but desertion was life-threatening. Because of these threats, no one was privy to these dark secrets. The primary, indwelling sin that I desperately needed to be saved from was fear. Fear owned me.

At no point in my stages of adolescence did I have control over my gender crisis or same-sex thoughts and feelings. In my experience, nothing seemed like a choice I could consciously choose. That had a massive influence on my perspective and pursuit of a resolution to the moral conflict.

Ironically, I felt safer as a masked Christian living in the dark with a forbidden longing and hidden identity than choosing to walk in the light as an open target.

4

FORSAKEN

Love never dies a natural death. It dies because we do not know how
to replenish its source. It dies of blindness and errors and betrayals.
It dies of illness and wounds; it dies of weariness,
of withering's, of tarnishing's.
Anais Nin

Shredded Tapestry

During my gender and sexual identity crisis, relationships within my village began to unravel, one thread at a time.

The thinnest tapestry thread that I intentionally cut was the connection with my biological mother. My mother was the parent I distrusted the most, and, as a result, was least invested in. As soon as my biological sisters were living their adult lives, I quickly ended my visitation rights with my mother. Unless I was going to be with my sisters, there was no real value in sustaining this turbulent relationship with my mother. This thought was not right, but it was what I opted to believe.

Although the other threads threatened were of a stronger hold and tighter bind, the first string that frayed was the relationship with my biological father. Spanning across a decade, my father's mental and physical health went into a downward spiral, starting with him losing control of his long-haul trucking business. After filing bankruptcy, he lost everything: his company, house, pick-up truck, and our recreational ski boat. The repossessions brought our annual family trips to an end. All of these events were happening around the same time our mother reappeared. After regaining a renewed relationship with our biological mother, the sustained relationship with our biological father was slowly melting away.

I believe bankruptcy took more than my father's material possessions. It stripped him of his identity and purpose. It was like he gave up his fight to live. He soon surrendered every waking moment of his days to chasing after his paranoid conspiracy theories. He believed that our country's federal government, as well as his own family, was out to kill, steal, and destroy him. He started spending endless hours, days, and years writing timestamped log entries of his most haunting thoughts and feelings. His stack of handwritten journals on odd pieces of paper became his prized possessions. Dad was enslaved to a world that no one could understand or break into.

Those closest to my dad came to the hard realization that he was suffering from a mental illness. His manic tantrums were becoming more episodic, unpredictable, and, at times, dangerous. There were some scary instances where my dad made life threats to immediate family members as well as strangers. People were beginning to complain about his erratic behavior. Someone had to intervene, or my dad would have eventually hurt himself or someone else.

The person who finally blew the whistle on our father was the one most affected: his girlfriend. Out of fear of her own safety and that of her sons, she pleaded with our closest relatives to help, and they responded. It was my aunts and uncles who regrettably admitted our father into the state's local mental asylum. Our father knew he needed help, but, like many, he was too prideful and afraid to admit it.

I was in junior high when I received the breaking news about Dad. Even though I was not surprised by the choice my relatives had to make, I was deeply affected by it. On the one hand, I was relieved that my dad was getting help, because I did not understand nor could rationalize his bizarre behavior. On the other hand, I was humiliated by where they were taking him and horrified by the pending prognosis. My classmates and I often made fun of the people living in the state's local mental hospital. We used to call the place the "looney bin". It sickened me to think I was now referring to my biological father. I was of his flesh and blood. If my dad was to be diagnosed as insane, I questioned my own mental stability.

After a few weeks of living in the mental asylum, my father begged his brothers and sisters to bail him out. Since Dad had served in the Army during the Korean War, they were able to admit him to the nearest Veteran's Health Administration Hospital as a qualified veteran. He was hospitalized and treated by the VHA psychiatric ward with schizophrenia. Then they diagnosed him with a bipolar disorder. The bipolar disorder seemed to be the most logical explanation of his manic highs and depressive lows. Dad suffered from his debilitating mental illness and the side effects of the prescribed medications. He had to take one pill to subdue or prevent the side effects of another. It was spirit-crushing to see him so heavily sedated. I could not decide which took away my father's quality of life more: the disease or the medications.

It was easier for me to resent the drugs and doctors rather than my dad. Although the VHA continuously treated our father, I never again saw the spirited, life-filled, childhood hero I once adored. I reluctantly had to face the inevitable truth. Dad was never going to be the father I longed for, and he was never coming back to rescue me. My dreams of ever getting to live with my dad were lost.

As I let go of one idolized father, I clasped onto my other father—J.W. My longing for J.W.'s affection intensified. Wherever he went, regardless of the day, time, or place, I wanted to go. I begged him daily to let me tag along. I tried to plead my case by stating how useful I could be or the work I could get done. He often gave a chuckling grin at some of my outlandish claims of performance. It was hard for anyone to take this 100-pound tomboy seriously when it came to hard, physical labor. On the days J.W. politely declined my services and left me behind, I patiently waited for his return. As soon as I saw his vehicle turning into his driveway, I sprinted out of the house to greet him.

During the days I did get to shadow J.W., I was at the height of my glory. Getting to ride on the farm machinery was better than any visiting carnival and their crazy rides. At his every command, I eagerly jumped to the task and willingly obeyed. I wanted nothing more than to please him. Since he was a man of few words and little patience, I could assume I had his approval if I had not been dismissed early or harshly reprimanded. Remaining in his presence was my targeted reward.

Not long after my father's mental health took its downward turn, there was a gradual decline in J.W.'s attitude and behavior. After Demi, Dawson, and Tiffany each graduated from high school and moved out of the home, J.W. seemed more agitated and disengaged. It was no secret that his number one vice was alcohol.

No one suspected him to be an alcoholic because he did not drink every day. However, we overlooked the more distinct pattern. He was clearly a binge drinker. He could go days, sometimes weeks, without touching an alcoholic drink. Yet, when he drank, the effects of alcohol took control and presented his dark side. His mood swings swayed back and forth between a passive depression or an outburst of explosive anger. Everyone loved the tenderhearted J.W., yet respectfully feared his wrath.

Now that I was a freshman in high school, and the only child still living at home, my attitude changed, too. It hardened mostly toward J.W. As his habits worsened, he began skipping one or two evening meals with Marilyn and me. On the nights he was late, Marilyn would always fix a hot plate of food and kept it warm in the oven until he returned. I knew when he was home because he always came through the back porch that adjoined my bedroom's east wall. When I heard the screeching sound of the screen door, I was relieved. Even though I was still glad to see him, I resented the fact he was so late. Plus, the time of return foretold his frame of mind. His foul moods usually corresponded to his lateness. I could not help but internalize J.W.'s behavior as a direct reflection of his lack of concern and love for me. I was not enough to keep his time or affection anchored.

There was one thread that remained intact, though, which was with Aunt Marilyn. She was my one constant that I could always count on.

Ultimate Desertion

By late spring, I was wrapping up my freshman year. It had been a good and accomplished year. I was one of the starting five on the high school women's basketball team who ranked in the district with high averages in scored points, assists, and rebounds. I excelled in track and field with my 440-yard run times and distances in long and triple jumps. I managed all this while maintaining a near-perfect GPA. I was making a name for myself.

On a Monday evening, Dawson called home and was elated to share his news. Knowing how I missed my childhood dog that had recently died from cancer, Dawson had found another blonde Cocker Spaniel puppy for sale. I was ecstatic at the thought of starting a brand-new relationship with another trustworthy companion. Even though it was a school night, Marilyn was willing to drive to the location of the puppy, about an hour and a half away. As soon as Marilyn and I finished our dinner, we headed out on our conquest, making a quick stop to pick up Demi on the way. I was hoping J.W. could go too, but it was one of those nights where he had not come home for dinner.

Once I laid eyes on the puppy, it was a done deal. As we headed home, I could hardly wait to surprise J.W. with my new puppy. When Marilyn pulled into our driveway around 10 p.m., J.W.'s garage was dark and empty. This time, I was more than disappointed with J.W.'s absence...I was steaming with anger. I was going to have to wait until the next morning to show off my new furry, four-legged sidekick.

Every morning, Marilyn was the first person up in the house. Her first task was preparing breakfast for J.W. Every day, Marilyn served his hot breakfast at the same place, in the same chair, and at the same time. What was strangely unusual that following morning was J.W.'s empty chair. He still had not come home. This was a new and peculiar behavior we had never witnessed. Worried and concerned, Marilyn went to look for him.

As Marilyn stepped out from the back porch and started walking toward J.W.'s garage about fifty yards away, she heard a faint rumbling sound. As she approached, she identified the sound as a running engine. Her hopes lifted. When Marilyn arrived at the doorway of the garage, she was startled to see the garage door was closed. J.W. never closed the garage door because it was a heavy, solid wood door that was difficult for even a grown man to open once it was shut. She yelled out his name, but there was no answer.

She panicked. Something was horribly wrong. All the weight of Marilyn's petite frame desperately tugged at the heavy garage door, but it would not budge. In a mad rush, she returned to our house, screaming my name. I quickly met her. The urgency in her shaky voice and the desperate look on her face sent chills up my spine. She hastily grabbed my arm and said, "Karol, I think there is something wrong with J.W."

We ran to the garage, and with joined strength pulled up on the door, but it did not move an inch. In sheer terror, Marilyn cried out, "I think J.W. is in there. We have to get in!"

Fear invoked adrenaline. There was only one other way in. I quickly ran around to the back of the garage and knocked out the window's glass with my bare hands. Once I had all of the glass pushed out, I jumped up and crawled through the window.

J.W.'s truck was parked inside, its engine idling. The driver's side door was open and the vehicle cab was empty. My eyes locked in on the white-socked feet of a human body lying beneath the driver's side door. The opened door was blocking the view of the person attached to the feet.

As I rushed around the door, I saw the entire body and face—it was J.W. He was lying still and on his back with his head positioned beneath the truck's exhaust pipe. His arms crossed his chest like he was taking a nap.

The fumes were suffocating, and my head felt dizzy and lightheaded. I had to step over his lifeless body to reach the cab of the truck and turn off the engine. I knew I needed to get J.W. out into fresh air as soon as possible. If I failed, Marilyn would have to recover two bodies.

After I had turned the truck engine off, I had to once again step around J.W. to make my way to the garage door. I fiercely tried to lift the door but failed. I grabbed a five-foot solid iron crowbar leaning in the corner of the garage and jabbed it beneath the garage door, pushing down with all my might. Finally, I saw a crack of daylight under the door. Then I saw Marilyn's fingers reaching under the door from the outside. Together, with her on one side and me on the other, we opened the door, and in came light and fresh air. As I tried to catch my breath, Marilyn lost hers as she looked at J.W.'s lifeless body. She immediately ran to the house and called for help.

All alone, I returned to J.W. I took hold of his arms and tried to lift him out of the garage. As I lifted his arms and his upper body, his head dropped back to the ground and his chest expelled a deep gurgling sound. The sound was horrifying. I feared I was hurting him. I just stood there, staring death in the face.

Once Marilyn returned, we both lifted J.W. and moved him outside of the garage. She tried to remain hopeful by telling me that the ambulance was on their way and would be there any minute. As I stood staring at his body, I could feel the life draining out of mine. I was about to pass out. Not taking my eyes off him, I slowly stepped away until my back touched a nearby tree. As my body slithered down the tree's trunk, I lost my senses. I could not see, think, feel, or move. My body went numb. Even if stabbed with a knife, I would not have felt any pain. My mind separated itself from my body.

I lost all sense of time. I do not remember if I waited thirty seconds or thirty minutes for the ambulance to arrive. When they did, they whisked J.W.'s body into the ambulance and rocketed out of our driveway with lights flashing and sirens blowing. The hospital was at least a twenty-minute drive away.

Everything was a blur. Marilyn and I ran back to the house as Demi arrived. Panic-stricken, Demi cried out, "Where is he? Where is Daddy?" I muttered, "He's dead." Demi refused to believe me. Marilyn ordered us to get in the car. I climbed into the back seat and silently stared out the window as I listened to the two of them clinging to hope. I already knew there was no hope. I had touched death. As I leaned my forehead onto the glass window, I felt the warmth of the sun on my face, but my body was ice cold. I would have been better off if I had died too. I was dead inside.

As soon as we entered the ER's waiting room, the doctors pronounced J.W. dead on arrival. Their words moved through me like a ghost—I felt spiritless. The man I worshipped for rescuing me had, in the end, forever deserted me. This devastating moment changed me, along with my perspective on everything: life, love, family, faith, and identity.

Just when I thought things could not get any worse, we lost another loved one. Four months after J.W.'s death, Marilyn's father died during open-heart surgery. I lost my beloved Grandpa and best friend. After receiving this heartbreaking news, I felt nothing. I could not cry or feel anything at all.

Our day-to-day living radically changed. My family life now consisted of one widow and one devastated child. We stayed on the farm until I finished my sophomore year, then Marilyn sold the farmhouse and we moved to my hometown. Oddly, we moved only blocks away from the home I was born in. My life went full circle.

For several months, Marilyn and I coexisted in a state of shock. Neither one of us have a full recollection of those two years. My entire sophomore year is a blur, except for a few good memories, like turning sixteen and buying my first car. Yet, during this time of shared trials and tribulations, Marilyn and I became unbreakable allies. We were two survivors walking a tightrope of hard times together. We held each other up and relied on each other to keep our sanity and life's balance. Marilyn having this dependency on me gave me a new sense of value and self-worth. This renewed purpose gave me at least one reason to keep living.

The Godforsaken Identity

Another casualty after J.W.'s death was my faith in God. God was now an enemy rather than a friend. Days after J.W.'s death, I stood outside, stared up at the

COMING OUT WITH CHRIST

sky, and screamed at God at the top of my lungs. I not only blamed God for taking J.W., but I blamed Him for everything that had happened to me, starting from birth.

After nearly passing out from the lengthy exhales and brief intakes, I stood in complete silence, waiting for God to respond. There was nothing. The clouds did not separate, lightning did not strike, nor did I hear a voice of thunder. God was silent, and that further fueled my animosity. Although my anger toward God did not change my belief in His existence, but it did make me deeply question His heart and character. I started to view God as this stone-cold ruler who sat on His throne in the heavens dictating rules and demanding costly allegiance while giving nothing in return. How could God be a nurturing God if he stripped infants from the breast of their mothers? How could God be a heavenly Father if he separated children from their earthly fathers? How could God be a good and compassionate God if he cursed a girl with a desire to be a boy? How could God be a fair and just God if he created homosexuality and then denied its existence? God left me with no alternative than to turn my heart against Him since He had unjustly turned His face from mine.

There was no purpose for the church, no trust in God, and no assurance of faith. The ultimate desertion not only came from my earthly fathers but, unimaginably, from my heavenly Father.

5

SAVED BY A KISS

If nothing saves us from death, may love at least save us from life.
Pablo Neruda

The First Kiss

At the vulnerable age of fifteen, I found myself drowning in a soul-crushing wave of tragedy and crisis. Over a brief time, I had lost all of my childhood heroes to incapacitating mental illnesses and physical death. As my body slowly awakened from shock, nothing could plug the gush of emotional pain. I would have preferred to suffer from severe, chronic pain than experience this infinite emotional pain. With physical pain, there is tangible evidence of the cause, followed by a prognosis for healing, however long. With emotional pain, the infliction is invisible, intangible, and everlasting. I did not know how to stop the bleeding, or where to turn for restoration and healing.

My reaction was to stuff down my feelings and emotions like the filling of a feathered pillow. If I stayed isolated and silenced, the feelings would eventually go away. There was no value or point in talking about them because no one could possibly understand or relate, or so I thought. That was what my past experiences of deep emotional pain had taught me. Like other unwanted feelings, I chose to compartmentalize these emotions. There were so many days and nights I hopelessly believed it would have been easier to die than to stay living. The belief of having everlasting love, joy, or happiness in my life felt forever lost.

Yet, I discovered a shimmer of hope in this encircling darkness. I stumbled upon a new origin of life from the most unlikely source, a newly kindled friendship.

A year before J.W.'s incident, I met a girl during the 4-H County fair. At first, I was caught off guard when out of a crowd of strange people, I heard someone call out my name. Margot was a confident extrovert who did not mind drawing attention to herself. That is how our distant friendship started, her pursuing me.

During my freshman year, we stayed in touch by writing letters. I usually received one or maybe two letters from Margot per week. A handwritten note or a phone call from a non-private telephone line were the only two methods of communication outside of seeing each other in person. Since it was during the school year, we occasionally saw each other in person at school-related conferences or sporting events. Every time we were together, it was a hoot. Margot was a prankster. She was always trying to trick or tease me about something. She was smart, savvy, and relentless. I had not had anyone persistently pursue me and my companionship outside of my mutual grade-school best friend and decoy boyfriend. Margot's friendship made me feel good about myself during a time I was struggling.

After Margot got word of J.W.'s death, she stood by my side. It was during that summer and early fall when my feelings grew for Margot, and I was finding myself wanting to be near her as much as possible. Letters were no longer appeasing my appetite. By my logic, my feelings were normal and innocent because she had become my dearest best friend. My grade-school best friend and I spent practically every waking moment together, either at school, during sleepovers, or on hour-long phone calls. This friendship appeared to be no different. Besides, all my previous best friends were consumed and monopolized by relationships with their steady boyfriends, so I needed a new best friend. Margot eventually broke up with her boyfriend, and I dropped mine, so we were both single and available.

In the beginning, this friendship was nothing special. That was what I kept telling myself until it slowly evolved into something more serious. When we were alone, our flirtatious interactions and nonverbal body language were emitting positive vibes. I was totally taken by Margot, as she was with me. We often competed in arm-wrestling matches to see who was the strongest. In reality, neither one cared about winning. What we really wanted was an acceptable way to touch one another while maintaining the safe zone.

As with every blossoming romance, whether gay or straight, the intensified feelings will ignite sexual behavior. We were friends for nearly two years before we confessed and yielded to our romantic feelings for one another. Our first bold move was finding every opportunity to hold hands. Drive-in theatres created the ideal space. We had all the privacy and darkness we needed to be close to each other without worrying who would see us.

I knew I was moving into unchartered waters when my body began to react to her touch. As we held each other's hand, my heart nearly pounded through my chest and the palms of my hands got clammy and sweaty. During the adrenaline rush, it was hard for me to not want more. I knew I was at a point of no return. By now, we both knew this relationship was taking us down an irreconcilable path, yet neither of us wanted to stop. My desires and needs quickly overruled the resistance created from morality. I was not going to let anything stand in the way.

At the end of one of our dates, I drove Margot home. Neither one of us wanted the night to end. As we sat in my car together talking well into the early morning hours, there was an undeniable moment of attraction. The desire to kiss her was consuming me, and nothing else in the world mattered. Even though I was risking rejection, I leaned in and kissed her. She consented. There was no turning back.

In fairy tales, they often tell stories about secret love potions that make people fall uncontrollably in love with one another. These love potions were able to take over people's free will. That was precisely how I felt after my first kiss with Margot. I felt spellbound for days after. Our secret same-sex relationship carried on for a year or so. For the longest time, we never told anyone else about what was going on in our relationship. Fear was the driving factor. We knew we were surrounded by judgmental, homophobic people. That was the norm for the era.

It was during this same-sex relationship that I felt most compelled to have a sex change. Although, the inner motives for the biological sex change shifted slightly. I wanted to marry Margot, and for that to happen in that day and age, I needed to become a man. I still wanted to be a man, but my motives were driven for reasons higher than my gender confusion. My fantasies were evolving into a reality, and that reality revolved around a real love for a real person who happened to be another woman.

As much as I understood love, I was crazy in love with Margot. She came into a period of my life when I thought I could never trust anyone or find love—and this relationship proved me wrong. Margot satisfied my starvation for acceptance and worthiness, and our romantic relationship consumed my heart, mind, and body. Her love was like honey, ever so sweet and filling.

As in any romantic relationship, sexual behavior became the next natural step toward an expression of deeper intimacy. I would have loved Margot regardless of the sexual contact, yet saying *I love you* was not enough to show her how much I loved her. Sexual behavior was a conduit for expressing our love for each other.

Human nature hungers and desires unfailing love. In Proverbs 27:7 (NLT), it says, "A person who is full refuses honey, but even bitter food tastes sweet to the hungry." Even though I knew this same-sex relationship was prohibited by the church and God, it quenched my insatiable thirst and ongoing hunger for love. This young Adam-like Eve was in love with another Eve. How could love be a sin? Since I felt God had abandoned me, there were little moral considerations left in this fight. Margot's affection far outweighed my perceived love of God. Why would I walk away from the one place I found love?

Margot was the first person outside of family and friends that gave me a purpose for living. Inevitably, I was saved by a forbidden kiss.

All good things must come to an end was undoubtedly a true statement for the depiction of my life. Less than two years after initiating our romance, Margot dumped me for another woman. To put the icing on the cake, she dared to callously deliver her news of infidelity on my eighteenth birthday. I do not know which of her actions I resented the most, her cheating on me with another woman, or breaking up with me on such a monumental day. Once more, love abandoned me.

My heart could only break to a certain point because it is impossible to re-break an already broken heart. It took me a couple of years to let go of Margot. It took a lifetime to let go of the effects of abandonment from both biological parents and my guardian parent, J.W. Later in life, my psychiatrist said, "The deeper the pain, the deeper the love." He spoke the truth. Emotional pain is proportionately measured by the depth of love.

What If?

After experiencing the devastating losses of loved ones, either by death, abandonment, or rejection, suicide became a dark-sided companion. Instead of respectfully fearing suicide, my suicidal thoughts began to comfort me. Unlike my same-sex attractions and gender identity confusion, suicide gave me a lot of choices. In my loneliest and darkest moments, I kept relapsing to "what if" suicidal thoughts. I would fill in each what-if statement with possible ways I could take my own life. What if I drove my car recklessly fast, and crashed and accidentally died? What if I played the pistol game of Russian Roulette? I wanted my death to appear accidental so it would bring less guilt, shame, and pain to the remaining family.

At the same time, it was family that led by example. If J.W. could commit suicide, then so could I. Dead or alive, he was still my hero. For several years after his suicidal death, the option to take my life felt tangible and doable.

Emerging Identity

By age eighteen, teenagers are actively exercising their free will. This was the time in my life where I was ready to declare my intention and choose my direction. It came down to one decision. Would I sacrifice love and fall back to the empty laws of God, the Church, and Christianity…or would I pursue my heart's passion, regardless of the pending condemnation?

Choosing to live among the living without love was choosing to live among the dead. For me, it was an unequivocal answer.

6

IN PURSUIT

You have your identity when you find out not what you can keep your
mind on,
but what you cannot keep your mind off.
A. R. Ammons

Worldly Goals

I had to make crucial decisions like every other high school graduate. I contemplated the repeated question, "What do I want to do with my life?" My public goals were to play collegiate basketball and move far away from the small-town environment. My individual goals were a different matter altogether. I knew what I wanted and where I needed to go to get it. Universally, what everyone desires is unfailing love. By the time I entered college, I knew I wanted to pursue women, exclusively. I expected to find unfailing love in my next same-sex relationship. Hopefully, the kind of relationship that would last a lifetime.

To pursue my heart's desire, my goal was to get lost in a city big enough that people did not know me. I shuddered at the thought of spending the rest of my life in a small town where everyone knew everyone's business and would pass judgment on my way of life. I did not want to wake up in the middle of the night with a burning cross in my front yard. Those things and a lot worse happened to those living as targeted minorities. For my safety and privacy, I was determined to move away to a city where I could unleash my desires and, ultimately, my sexual identity.

However, love was not going to pay the cost of higher education. Financially, I was on my own. The same college that recruited me to play Division II Women's basketball offered a minor academic scholarship. Even though I had to try out as a walk-on for the women's basketball team, I knew the scouting coaches had recognized my potential. I was at least hopeful in making the team.

Destiny had a different plan. Just days before the scheduled tryouts, I rolled my right ankle while scrimmaging with a few high school teammates. The severe sprain and possible hairline fracture had me walking on crutches for my first few weeks of college. After finalizing tryouts and selecting her walk-ons, the head coach assured me I would have made the team. She encouraged me to stay inspired and in shape and said I could maybe practice with them in the upcoming offseason. I was counting on every word she spoke.

The following year, the university promoted women's basketball from a Division II to a Division I league, along with a newly recruited head coach who knew nothing about me. This promotion changed everything. The caliber of women players was much taller, physically stronger, and more talented than my ability. After playing basketball for over a decade, the game was over.

I continued to worry about how I would pay for college. My first year of expenses were covered by my academic scholarship and Aunt Marilyn, but I had no idea how I was going to pay for the next three years. Then I got a gracious surprise. My dad was granted a full-time disability pension through the U.S. Veteran's Administration agency, and he mailed me a short handwritten letter with an enclosed personal check written out to my name. The check's memo said, "for college". I didn't know my father knew I was going to college or how he got my address. Miraculously, the check amount covered the entire cost of one semester, including tuition, books, and most of my living expenses.

He continued to send a personal check twice a year until I graduated three years later. It was a blessing to both of us. I believe this opportunity gave my father a sense of purpose and redemption. His generosity gave us a renewed connection.

I wanted to be a good steward of my dad's money, so I was in hot pursuit of a career field that jived with my personality and would make a palatable living. Now that basketball was utterly out of reach, I was on track to starting a new career and new life in a city far, far away.

To narrow the choices of career paths, I quickly eliminated everything I despised. Time and time again, each disliked career choice pointed toward a straightforward truth—I did not want to help or work with people. My hostility toward people came out of fear and distrust. If they knew that I loved women instead of men, I would be hated, discriminated against, and possibly harmed. This was in the early '80s, during the publicized AIDS epidemic where homosexuals were primarily considered detestable, marginalized outcasts.

As I finished my general electives, I was hoping something would click and I would magically know what field of study to choose. Finding a career that eliminated people limited my options. Time was running out as I entered my junior year with an undeclared major. I boiled down my top choices to three areas: geology/geography, psychology, and religion.

With psychology, I was seeking answers to the causes of homosexuality. I wanted to know why I was sexually attracted to women instead of men, and why I was secretly wishing to be a man. I enrolled in several courses, but I still came up with no rock-solid answers. I managed to receive extra credit in my entry-level psychology courses by volunteering for one-on-one counseling with the psychology graduate students doing their internships. I had nothing to lose because these sessions were confidential. I discovered that I got a lot more out of these sessions than extra credit. After I spilled my guts, telling this stranger everything, including how I felt toward women, my burdens were unexpectedly lighter. Telling someone all of my darkest secrets, and knowing they were not judging me for them, gave me a sense of healing. That graduate student had no idea how much she had helped me in just a few hours of listening intently.

I gravitated toward religion because I still believed in God and I was intrigued by God's written word. Even nonbelievers know that the Bible is written about God, whether they choose to accept or follow what it says. I was fascinated more by the archeology of religion. These archaeological finds were visible evidence that the Bible's stories did take place. Our classroom discussions were based on factual content, not morality. I wanted to know more about the content of the Bible but not to live by it. My truth did not allow to me live by God's truth.

I discovered the mother lode in my geology/geography studies. This path of studies quickly led me to a new and alluring field study called Cartography & Map Technology. I fell in love with rocks and routes. The United States Department of

Defense recruited nearly every cartography/geography graduate from my college. My future looked bright and my career was about to take off. This choice in a major unequivocally met all my requirements, including love in a city, a good salary, and the elimination of working with people. I loved rocks, not people.

Gender Contentment

The other positive growth that came out of my four collegiate years was learning to reconcile my differences with my gender identity. I was finding myself more satisfied with expressing my gender as a woman. My gender identity was aligning closer to my biological sex. In simpler terms, I was feeling more comfortable and confident in being a woman—inside and out.

My gender identity satisfaction emerged from the positive affirmation that came from other people, especially those closest to me. Increased positive affirmations lowered my masculinity and elevated my femininity. There was a definite correlation. Men and women alike, gay or straight, were attracted to me. As I grew out my hair and wore make-up and earrings, people took notice. I was turning heads, so to speak. I was so hungry for attention that I embraced and accepted my femininity just to get it. Most people feel better about themselves when others speak with loving words of affirmation and encouragement. I was living proof of Pavlov's psychological laws of human conditioning. I wanted more of what sounded good. People's positive attention boosted my self-esteem and body image and led me to believe that being a woman had its advantages.

I kept inching closer and closer to my femininity with softer, effeminate gender expression. Ironically, the same child that regularly cried and fussed about her long, curly hair was now sporting a long, curly perm.

It is essential to understand that while I was more satisfied with my female gender expression, it had no impact on the direction of my same-sex feelings, attractions, and sexual identity. Most lesbians who dated women exclusively were usually unattracted to men. If I became a man, most lesbians would have rejected me. It was no longer necessary or financially practical to change my body to a man's body just because I liked women. My mind agreed with the fact that women liked me and wanted me as a woman. It was a breakthrough, so to speak.

The other rationale that kept me as a woman was the fact that heterosexual women liked men only. Even if I transitioned from a woman to a man and became a trans man, I would not be able to compete with men and their innate biological sex. Once a heterosexual woman realized she was dating a woman, she would end the relationship. Again, more potential rejection.

I mentally opted out of my expressed masculinity and partially embraced my femininity. I proudly accepted my new identity: a lipstick lesbian. I still predominantly fantasized about being a man, but it remained just that—a fantasy.

Nevertheless, my resignation toward my gender identity did not free me of my deep resentment toward men. I still coveted men because they were born as men and could freely and naturally love women in all aspects: physiologically, psychologically, emotionally, and physically. They possessed the whole package. I believed that they arrogantly took advantage of women and abused their powers. The way I saw men treating and disrespecting women infuriated me. My hatred toward men became a stewing pot, especially with the men who were winning the hearts of the women I secretly desired.

No two transgender people are alike, and neither are their experiences and stories. Transgenderism is a rare and complex subject, and what I have shared in this story has taken me years to understand and explain. I struggled with my gender identity for the first quarter-century of my life, and not once did I feel I could consciously stop or reroute my thoughts and feelings. I am grateful that I stumbled upon an alternative path early on. Not every transgender person will find such an easy way out.

Sexual Identity

By age twenty-three, as a cum laude graduate with a Bachelor of Science degree in the field of Cartography & Map Technology, I was sure of who I was and what I wanted out of life. I was an inwardly affirmed, yet outwardly closeted, lesbian pursuing a career that avoided people. I kept my sexual identity in the closet by intentionally hiding it from my heterosexual friends and family. My attitude was that who I loved and how I loved them was nobody's business but my own. I believed everyone had a right to find love, and there should be no judgment or condemnation in where they went to find it.

How I got to this point of clarity and acceptance with my sexual identity took nearly a decade of processing my feelings, emotions, sexual attractions, and sexual behavior, compounded by positive and negative experiences. One truth I commonly share with others today is the fact that the time from the initial discovery of same-sex attractions, to acting on the sexual behavior, to finally labeling and declaring the sexual identity, takes years. When a person confides in someone concerning their same-sex attractions or bisexual identity, they have confidence in knowing that they did not come to that conclusion overnight. Their story will most likely have spanned years, and, potentially, started very early in life.

At no point in this process of discovery did I feel I had any control over my same-sex feelings and attraction. Back when I was eleven and twelve years old, the last thing I wanted was to be targeted differently than everyone else. My broken childhood already marginalized me as an outcast. If I could have flipped a switch and reoriented my gender identity and sexual identity, I would have flipped it without any hesitation. Yet, there was no magical lever to pull or wand to wave that could redirect my mind or my feelings. Although I did not create my homosexuality, I did choose to embrace it. If I could not change who I was, then I felt I had no other choice than to accept it.

7

OUT OF HIDING

Man is not what he thinks he is, he is what he hides.
Andre Maraux

Gay Declaration

After graduating as one of the top students in the field of Cartography & Map Technology, I was on track to meeting all job applicant requirements for the Department of Defense's Mapping Agency. Every week after applying, I checked the mailbox, anxiously awaiting my package. When the package finally arrived, I was surprised at the volume of papers I had to fill out.

I pulled out this 8 x 11" booklet. It was neon pink, which I thought was a rather flamboyant choice for the DOD. The booklet's cover clearly and boldly stated the document's importance. It read something like this:

ALL QUESTIONS CONTAINED IN THIS BOOKLET
MUST BE ANSWERED COMPLETELY,
OR APPLICATION WILL BE DISREGARDED.

I could not imagine that there was anything else to ask after reviewing all the other background information requested. As I opened the pink booklet, I turned to the first page. It had a single question at the top.

> *Have you ever claimed or filed for bankruptcy? If yes, please provide details.*

Several blank pages followed the first page to give the person ample space to write out all the details. I was so relieved because this was an easy question to answer. I wrote a single word answer: "No."

Then I flipped through the blank pages and found the second question. My hands began to tremble and my heart started pounding.

> *Have you ever participated in a homosexual act? If yes, please provide details.*

How could they ask such a private question? What did my sexuality have to do with making maps?

There was no skirting around the question or my answer because I was guilty. I could not decide what they meant by details, though. Where did I start and where did I end? What constituted as a homosexual act? Did it mean holding hands, kissing, etc.? Or, how often? Once? Twice? I never thought to count the number of acts. There were not enough instructions or blank pages to unravel these kinds of details. It was a preposterous question.

Should I lie or tell the truth? Both decisions were risky with serious, life-altering consequences. If I lied, I would have to continue living in secrecy…from the federal government. Falsifying a federal document is a felony and a career smasher.

If I told the truth, my career would end before it ever started. There was a high probability that the United States Federal Government would reject an affirmative answer. Or, at a minimum, intentionally place my application at the bottom of the pile. There had to be strategic reasons for separating and highlighting these two distinct questions in bright neon pink. The booklet was probably the first piece of information reviewed in order to easily reject applicants.

I procrastinated this fateful decision as long as I could. I waited until I had everything finished and prepared to mail. I kept weighing the pros and cons. It came down to two competing factors. If I told the truth, I would be throwing away my college education and career. If I lied, I would be living in the closet for years to come.

Weeks passed after I submitted my application. I checked the mailbox every single day. After a few months passed, I gave in and contacted the designated representative to find out why it was taking so long for them to process my application. She checked my application status and then gave me the bad news. My acceptance letter had returned to them via postal mail. They had to follow their protocol, and all returned postal mail was an automatic rejection. Unfortunately for me, after graduation, I had moved to another address, and I never thought to notify them of my new address. A costly mistake.

There was more bad news. The Defense Mapping Agency had gone into a hiring freeze. I said aloud, "Are you kidding me?" She politely said, "I am sorry, but we will be hiring again in maybe two or three years." In two or three years?

I was out of college, out of work, and out of money. To add to the humiliation, I had to return to my claustrophobic and homophobic hometown. I know it is not uncommon for unemployed college graduates to move back in with their parents, but it is a bit more challenging for a closeted lesbian.

However, the federal recruiter was right. Precisely three years after my "return to sender" incident, I got a chance to redeem myself.

I again anxiously waited for the application package. As soon as it arrived, I ripped through it. I had to know if the neon pink booklet was inside. I took every piece of paper out of the large envelope and laid them out on my kitchen table. I let out a sigh of relief. The package did not have anything asking any dreaded questions about my sexuality. I quickly filled out the bundle of forms and, with confidence, mailed my application.

I finally received my acceptance letter. My first day of employment at the Defense Mapping Agency was set for the following month. I rented the smallest U-Haul, packed all my belongings, and headed to St. Louis, Missouri. It was not my first choice in cities, but it was a large city that was far enough away.

I launched into my first day of federal employment with other entry-level cartographers. It was quite a diverse group, with men and women from all over the United States.

At one point in our orientation, they took us into a large room and had us sit at individual desks. They then handed us a multiple page questionnaire with multiple choice answers. As I answered the questions, I came to a screeching halt. There was that dreaded question again. The only thing different about the question asked this go-round was the fact it was a multiple-choice answer. It read, *"Have you ever participated in a homosexual act?"* and was followed by *"yes or no".* At least it was a simple answer that did not require details.

Yet I was faced with another test of integrity, honesty, and character. Was I going to tell the government the truth?

I had spent the last three years struggling with my previous decision to lie. I was twenty-six years old and tired of hiding my secret life. If I lost my job, so be it. I circled "yes", then finished the remaining questions and handed in my questionnaire. One word put everything on the line. My reputation, my secrets, my past same-sex relationships, my career...but I was ready to stop running.

I honestly expected armed guards to handcuff me and escort me out the front door like a criminal. I was bracing for the humiliation and wishing I had not already unpacked my U-Haul trailer. This was going to be an interesting conversation with my family, but there was no turning back now.

Then they called out my name. I boldly stood up and acknowledged myself. The administrative woman said, "Follow me, please." All eyes were on me as I followed the woman out of the room.

As I walked into a tiny office space, I saw nothing but four blank walls, no windows, and a small desk covered in piles of paper. There was one empty chair facing her desk. As she closed the door behind me, she asked me to take a seat.

The only thing between this woman and me was a small desk and a typewriter. She looked down as she positioned her fingers on the typewriter keys, then said, "Give me all the details of your homosexual acts." This left me dumbfounded for a few seconds. Attempting to buy time to think, I blurted out, "What details are you looking for?" Then the interrogation began. When did the acts occur? All actions. With whom had I performed the acts? I had to give names of the person(s) involved. I was shocked by the line of questioning. How were these details relevant? Why was it not enough to say that I was a lesbian? Then it hit me. Dirty secrets become governmental spies' bargaining chips.

I bit my tongue. Was this all necessary for me to be a cartographer? For heaven sakes, I was only going to be making maps. I was not going to become a foreign diplomat or acting U.S. Secretary of State. As I subjectively gave out details, I kept wondering if I was the only new hire who was telling the whole truth and nothing but the truth. Were there any others that were hiding skeletons in their closets? Was homosexuality considered the only risky behavior to the federal government? I was suspicious that this was a cover-up for the federal government to quietly screen out all sexual minority people.

In a blend of anger and fear, I confessed every homosexual act I chose to reveal in enough detail that seemed to appease her. She typed out every one of my statements while showing no emotion or concern with what she was putting me through. I was a case file, not a person. After she finished typing the document, I signed an affidavit. At last, she looked me straight in the eyes and commented, "If you want to obtain your top-security clearance, which is required to keep your job here, I strongly suggest you come out to at least your family."

The next step was inevitable.

It was a turning point. I opened my closet door, walked out into the daylight, and publicly declared my homosexual identity to my closest family members and friends.

After waiting for nearly a decade to come out, the outcome was favorable. I was relieved that no one in my family ousted me from their lives. However, this was when I learned the difference between tolerance, acceptance, and approval. Some tolerated me but despised the concept and behavior of homosexuality. Some accepted me without approval just to prevent losing their relationship with me. Some feared for my salvation. All in all, I was fortunate because no one rejected or abandoned me, and they conditionally accepted me. I was okay with that because I never expected their approval. Acceptance and approval hold different expectations.

The fight with the federal government was just getting started. Our class of new hires went through extensive cartographic onsite training for several weeks. At the end of our training, DMA assigned all cartographic graduates without top-secret security clearances to the "holding tank". The holding tank work was completing odds-and-ends tasks while waiting for security clearances.

Day by day, week by week, month by month, I watched every new hire from my graduating class launch into their careers. It was humiliating and embarrassing for a top cartographic student to remain in the holding tank. After telling my peers the single reason behind the federal delay, most had empathy. They did not agree with the waiting game.

Although held in this holding pattern with my career, the process of coming out unleashed personal freedom. I could finally live out my newly proclaimed identity. It opened me to a whole new world of other LGBTQ people and their support. Taking a stand for my lesbian status and fighting against the federal government gave me more self-confidence. I had the attitude of "Bring it". I was standing for my gay rights. By now, I believed this was blatant discrimination by the federal government and against my equal rights as a U.S. Citizen, but there was one looming reality. No state or federal law was protecting gay rights. In most states, any employee, government or private, could fire a person just for being gay. I was still in danger of losing this fight, and I was in the battle all alone.

The FBI was still actively conducting a background investigation into me and my past, and I was assigned a special FBI Agent. He contacted and interviewed me several times, saying he wanted to grant justice and give a fair assessment into my unique circumstances. Of course, I believed him; he was an FBI Agent.

There seemed to be another motive behind his justice, though. In one of our private interviews, the FBI Agent lifted and placed his briefcase upon his desk, unsnapped the latches, and lifted the top open. Then he asked, "Do I need to get out the knee pads?" It took me a few seconds to register what he was implying. After I caught his sexual innuendo, I gagged! This man was an idiot for asking a lesbian to perform a sexual act on a man. Not until hell froze over! This was sexual harassment. Although my blood pressure skyrocketed and I wanted to punch the guy, I had to remain calm. I was determined now more than ever to beat this case.

I politely responded, "No. There is no need for those." I was at his mercy. The agent kept pursuing me for days. He took it as far as inviting himself into my home and interviewing me and my new girlfriend at the time. I saw a darker side in the internal operations of the government toward minorities, LGBTQ members, and females. I will never know for sure if he was pursuing facts, me, or bargaining some sexual act in exchange for my security clearance. I rapidly lost all faith in men and trust in our federal government.

Two years and two months after my date of hire, the federal government finally granted me my top-secret security clearance. Consequently, I was behind my peers by two pay grades, costing me thousands of dollars yearly.

I paid the price of a forerunner, but I paved the way for life, liberty, and equality for other LGBTQ employees in the federal workforce.

It is ironic how our U.S. Declaration of Independence starts as:

We hold these truths to be self-evident, that all men are created equal, that they are endowed by their Creator with certain unalienable Rights, that among these are Life, Liberty, and the pursuit of Happiness.

Uncle Sam granted me more than a civilian's high-security clearance. The federal government gave me equal rights to life, liberty, and the pursuit of happiness as a gay employee. Who knew that our human sexuality could be such a powerful tool of treason?

Gay Identity

My newly declared gay identity took on a life of its own. Through my same-sex experiences, I was getting what I had longed for—integrity, love, acceptance, and a sense of belonging. I wanted to be true to my feelings, and that gave me integrity. I wanted to love, and in women, I found it. I wanted to belong, and in the LGBTQ community, they welcomed me. I wanted to be known and accepted, and that gave me my gay identity.

However, there was a hefty price tag attached to my gay identity. What I did not realize then was how the gay identity staked out territory beyond my sexuality. My gay pride began to subconsciously and consciously influence personal decisions such as career, passions, friends, family, clothes, men, where I chose to live, and, lastly, my attitude toward Christians and God. I generalized and judged all Christians as gay-haters and God as their Headship. Church had become a full-on enemy, personal threat, and a barrier to my love and happiness.

Because of my gay identity, I soon built a thirty-foot wall of my own to keep what I loved in and what I hated out. Speaking from my heartfelt regret, building any border or barrier comes at a divisive cost far higher and broader than time, materials, and labor. Because of my gay identity, I began pushing all people, good and bad, away based solely on their attitudes and beliefs about homosexuality and my way of life. I began to isolate and alienate close friends and family members as an enemy and threat. Ironic, is it not? A child who endlessly struggled with wanting to be loved, accepted, and valued became her own worst enemy. Regardless of sexuality, gender, race, or religion, built walls, at any height, will always come with an enormous price.

8

GAY IS OKAY

We can be redeemed only to the extent to which we see ourselves.
Martin Buber

Banner of Pride

I was out and proud! After spending ten years secretively hiding my love for women, by age twenty-six, my gay identity had finally liberated me. Nothing stood in the way of achieving my long-awaited freedom, love, and happiness.

I was ready to indulge in all my heart's desires and what my mind could not stop thinking about—everlasting love and personal happiness. Being same-sex-attracted should never deny a person a life of wholeness and happiness. Is it not our inherited right as human beings? Happiness is our life's primary purpose. With this kind of thinking, my sexuality became my life's source of authority over everything, including spirituality and morality.

This declaration of gay independence was crucial to my newfound integrity and identity. My pleasure came from women and women only. By overcoming fears of rejection after fully disclosing myself to those I loved, I was committed to owning and proving the importance of my gay identity to the world.

To exonerate my gay identity, I identified myself as an exclusive same-sex-attracted lesbian. It was crucial for me to protect the purity of lesbianism because I soon discovered that I was a minority among the minority in my close-knit lesbian community. In my inner circle of same-sex-attracted women, few women experienced gender confusion to the extent I had. All my lesbian friends seemed to be fully content and satisfied with their female gender. Another confusing and frustrating factor among my lesbian friends were their bisexual tendencies. Some same-sex-attracted women confessed to their varying degrees of sexual attraction to women and men. It enraged me because I saw it as a betrayal of lesbianism. Now that I was out of the closet, I was a lesbian purist. It was all or nothing. My hardline lesbianism made me stand out in my inner circle of gay friends. I became a hardcore lesbian and a gay advocate that demanded a certain degree of loyalty from every same-sex-attracted woman. I had no room for leniency toward any differences in beliefs. My self-righteous opinions and judgmental thoughts further marginalized me.

Despite my rigid standards and expectations of LGBTQ people, I stayed steady in the hope of finding perfect love. Perfect love meant unconditional, unfailing, and abiding love that met all my needs and completed me. Perfect love was out there, and I was determined to find it.

Despite my efforts, love kept eluding me. After ten years of pursuing same-sex relationships, I came up with nothing. Without love, life was utterly meaningless. After celebrating my gay independence for three brief years, I was in another soul-crushing crisis.

I kept asking, "Why? Why can I not find love? Am I not loveable?" The internal voices kept bombarding me with their endless, negative chatter. The one glaring fact I could not deny was that I was the common denominator. Something had to be wrong with me. Each rejection cut me open and a little deeper. My failed attempts at finding unfailing love was causing me to bleed out. Each letdown was a reliving of past betrayals. The rise in emotional pain was becoming unbearable.

After losing my emotional grip, I spiraled deep into depression and anxiety. I dropped twenty pounds in a matter of weeks. My tall, slender physique of lean muscle barely covered my bones. Sporadic and uncompromising panic attacks were quickly withering my mind and body.

I fiercely denied that I needed professional help. After witnessing the physical and mental struggles of my past idols, Dad and Uncle J.W., I was not going to succumb to their fate or a diagnosis.

The unpredictable panic attacks kept me imprisoned. I did not want people to see me in this state of mind, so I avoided contact with nearly everyone and barricaded myself indoors with my most trusted companions: my dogs.

In one of my lockdowns, I became desperate to find some glimmer of hope that this chapter of my life would end, one way or another. I grabbed the Bible that my church had gifted me at my high school graduation. I was frantic to find encouragement, courage, and strength to keep me afloat during these low tides. After flipping pages, I stopped, and, from the left page to the right, I scanned, looking for words of comfort. Immediately, three words popped out. I had to capture this wisdom, so I grabbed a piece of paper and wrote down three words.

Faith, hope, and love. I kept reciting my written words, hoping I would believe they were true. These words were telling me to hang tight and keep feeling, but the one word that was the hardest to accept was the greatest of these—love.

My heart refused to believe in the last word, so I rejected all three of them. I was a fool to think anything written in the Bible would help me. I crushed my handwritten note into a wad and tossed it into the tall kitchen trash can. I collapsed onto my bed and cried uncontrollably. It was hopeless.

My most recent partner and I had adopted a puppy that we named Ditto. Ditto was our parental trial before attempting to have our own children. It was the break-up with this adulterous partner that had left me spiraling out of control.

After I'd been crying for some time, Ditto jumped up on the bed and stood over me, cocking her head to one side. I don't think she had ever heard me cry before, so the sound intrigued her. Then she dropped something out of her mouth, and it fell on my chest. It was the wadded piece of paper. How had she retrieved this out of the trash? Why had she decided to bring it to me? Her behavior went beyond coincidence. I believed it was God trying to get my attention. Even though I could not fully accept the truth of these three words yet, I did believe in God's ability to hear my outcries. After fifteen long years, my attitude toward God began to change.

Even though I felt God was with me, He did not take away my problems or pain. My anxiety and depression continued to consume all of me, day by day, breath by breath. To me, mental illness was personal and represented abandonment, failure, and rejection. It haunted my mother, my father, and Uncle J.W., and it destroyed my family.

One of my accountability partners who was in her own battle with suicidal thoughts and depression suggested using art to express and release my toxic energy. At this point, I was desperate to try anything except professional help.

Maybe art would work. I needed an image that would depict inspiration and hope as a roadmap of where I was and where I wanted to go. I wanted to capture the state of my heart from its starting place to its destination: a resurrected heart from pain and suffering to love and joy. Every heart represented the stages of a healing journey, with each background color representing a perspective of transformation.

I proudly signed my inspired work of art (now portrayed on this book's front cover) with my initials, framed it, and hung it in my living room. Every day I passed by this framed image, I tried to imagine what it would feel like to have a fully healed heart filled with faith, hope, and love.

Self-Redemption

After turning thirty, my life was at an all-time low. While the world was celebrating the coming of the next new year, I was struggling to find a reason to stay alive. Like a caged animal, I was anxiously pacing back and forth in my apartment, trying to escape anxious feelings of depression. I was defeated by the bombarding thoughts of wanting to take my own life. In desperation, I called for help. I reached out to two close friends who had heard rumors of my most recent break-up. They were two trustworthy and supportive lesbian friends who faithfully believed in God. Knowing they were believers in God gave me comfort.

Once they opened their front door and saw my face, they insisted that I spent the night. I could no longer disguise my fear and desperation. As the evening went on, I became edgy and restless. As I felt another panic attack coming on, I locked myself in the guest bathroom. My legs could no longer support my body's weight, so I fell to the floor and laid in a fetal position. *I cannot live like this anymore, God. I cannot live in this constant fear of being alone.* I wanted to die so my anxiety would stop permanently.

Then I heard a different voice. It asked me, "Are you going to quit like your dad and uncle?" It had to be the voice of God, because only God knew the powerful impact behind such a poignant and personal question. His words resonated with my broken heart from rejection by the two men I loved most. God was right. How could I allow myself to do what I condemned these two men for doing? How would

I be any better of a person? So, I answered. *God, I do not want to quit on life, but I can no longer live like this, and something has to give and give now.*

Then a gentle knock on the door interrupted my conversation with God. I unlocked the door and my friends opened it. In a weak, trembling voice, I whispered, "I can't live like this anymore. I don't know how I am going to get through this." One of my friends said, "Let us take a walk outside together and get some fresh air. It will help clear your mind."

Walking in the late hours of the Midwest's chilly and damp January weather was invigorating, but not enough to distract me from my mental chaos. My friends lived in a beautiful custom-built home on the outskirts of a St. Louis suburb. At the crest of their property, there was a breathtaking view of the sprawling city lights. I could feel a wintry mist touching my face as I tried to take in the stunning views. My single-mindedness kept returning to the gripping thoughts of fear, despair, and hopelessness.

Under my breath, I repeatedly whispered, "I cannot do this anymore, God." I then heard an audible voice that gently whispered in my ears, "It will be okay." I turned to my friends and asked, "Did you hear that?" They both replied, "Hear what?" I told them, "Someone just said to me, 'It will be okay.'" They were both oblivious to the voice I had just heard. Their logical comeback was, "Of course, it will be okay," discounting the possibility of another voice. I had recognized the negative voices, yet this voice was quite different. This voice gave me instantaneous comfort.

The voice immediately drew me nearer to God. I turned to my friends and spoke a remarkable new truth that I now believed. "Guys, I am going to be okay. I am going to get through this." Within a split second, the Light penetrated the darkness and lifted my spirit out of the muck. Only the Almighty God and His Holy Spirit could breathe life into a hopeless soul. It was a supernatural encounter with the Holy Spirit that I could hardly articulate but believed wholeheartedly.

Coming down from the hillside was a complete turnaround from the climb up. It was like I had a Mt. Sinai experience like Moses in the Old Testament. My spellbound mind and spirit were now filled with hope that everything would be okay. God gave me a promise of deliverance—I would eventually break out of this darkness, but it would be a long journey. Most importantly, this hope gave me the desire to stay alive. Even though I was physically alone and hurting emotionally, I had renewed faith that my God was not only with me but was rooting for me.

My next day was a brand-new day. The voice I heard awakened me to some facts I had to face about myself. I needed to reevaluate my way of life and turn in a new direction. I needed and wanted to live right for God. It meant I needed to rid myself of some bad habits and create new, positive ones. As I started to take a hard look within, I was ready to do some major housecleaning.

One thing I was confident I did not need to change was my sexual identity. My self-assessment concluded that the demons I was fighting had nothing to do with my homosexuality. I wholeheartedly believed I was having a relational crisis, not a sexual crisis. There was no correlation.

However, many other aspects of my life were subject to change. I could no longer run from my mental health issues. My mind had become my worst enemy. I knew I needed professional help. I had one stipulation in finding a counselor. My therapeutic counselor had to be gay affirming. The last place I was going to go was Christian counseling because I believed they would say my only problem was homosexuality and that if I would abandon my homosexual practice and turn to heterosexuality, it would cure me. Heterosexuality did not mean holiness. My problems were not sexual problems…they were typical life problems.

I finally submitted myself to professional therapeutic help. To my surprise, my new counselor won me over in fifteen minutes. That was a miracle because I came in with boxing gloves on. I even gave her an ultimatum in the first five minutes. If her diagnosis hinted to any mental disorder in need of medication, I was not coming back. I told her I would kill myself before I followed that path. She calmly and patiently listened until I stopped ranting and then gently said something like, "Okay. Let's talk about it." Not only did her gentle voice comfort me, but the way she looked into my eyes and listened gave me warmth and encouragement. I could not recall the last time someone leaned in and paid close attention to me without asking for something in return. My counselor was a loving wife and mother of two children, one a gay son. She was exactly what I needed, though I didn't recognize the need.

My counseling sessions lasted five years. I came to realize that if I spent thirty years imprisoned by my mind's unhealthy beliefs about myself, then getting these things straightened out in five years was like an early parole.

Extended counseling brought about other positive life changes, too. I was slowly coming out from under my rock and stepping boldly into my core identity. I was finding self-worth and value from within, rather than outside of myself. I adapted to positive thinking and good habits. I started street running, which increased my appetite and cleared my mind. I made a significant decision to quit self-medicating my emotional pain with alcohol. I called it my emotional sobriety. I needed to experience my raw feelings without numbing them with alcohol. All these decisions were having a positive impact on my mind, body, and spirit.

The last positive change that came from my experience was my desire to return to God and church. I felt I owed God something in return for saving my life. I decided to go back to church as a sacrificial act to earn God's approval, not the approval of Christians. I had no interest or concern with appeasing Christians…they were still the enemy.

I wanted back in God's grace. I felt what displeased God most was my days of drunkenness, lustfulness, anger, jealousy, greed, and, lastly, my sexual practices outside of marriage. When I heard God's voice, He said, "It will be okay." He did not say, "It will be okay as long as you are not gay." There were no conditional clauses. God was pursuing my heart rather than my sexuality.

As God promised, my life was back on track, and things were going great. I was thriving in my revived life and wholeness. It was time to test my righteousness to see if I had earned God's next reward—my heart's greatest desire, a lifetime partner (wife) and family.

I thought my prayers were answered when I met my lifetime partner and fell in love once again. She was smart, attractive, and, most importantly, willing to be faithful. After our first year together, we exchanged wedding vows and rings, which, to me, meant we were officially married. Legalized same-sex marriage was still years away. Our newly merged family consisted of a total of five four-legged children. We were the Brady Bunch.

At age thirty-six, life was good, and Jamie and I were writing new chapters of our lives. I felt God was blessing us monetarily with the purchases of three new homes, cars, boats, and lucrative careers in the beautiful northwest region of the United States. We also discovered a gay-affirming church, and, for the first time in my life, I officially joined as an openly affirmed gay Christian. Life could not have been better. I had everything that made me happy.

Then came the next chain of extraordinary events. We had a change of heart concerning children and having a family. One of my best friends had adopted a newborn, and I immediately fell in love with her. My friend nicknamed me the "baby swooper" because if anyone laid the baby down, I would come along and swoop the baby up in my arms.

Jamie and I talked it over for a few months and did some research on adoption. We first considered out-of-country adoptions, but it was expensive, with no guarantee that other countries would support same-sex couples as adoptive parents. The thought of adopting a child and then losing custody because of our lifestyle was not an option. With my abandonment issues, I was going to make sure that under any circumstances, I would not lose my kid.

That led us to our next option: getting pregnant and having our own child. Our first big question was if there were any local fertility clinics that would provide services to a same-sex couple. We were living in a conservative state with many religious affiliations. Despite the odds, we found a well-known and respectable clinic that was willing to provide fertility services to a same-sex couple. A door opened.

After our first visit to the fertility clinic, we had to face another harsh reality—age does matter when it comes to fertility. Our most viable and practical option was in vitro fertilization (IVF), although, statistically, the percentage of getting pregnant over the age of forty was much lower than I had anticipated.

Then we had to decide which one of us would carry the child. My concerns about a midlife pregnancy were more about my gender identity than my age. The wife, not the husband, gets pregnant, and I still thought of myself more like the husband in our relationship. There was another hidden motive that weighed heavier on my mind, though. I could not bear the thought of falling in love with this child and then possibly losing the child to the surrogate mother in a divorce. State law at the time did not recognize same-sex parents on the child's birth certificate. The surrogate mother had all the parental rights of the child. I did not necessarily doubt our marriage, but I feared losing my child if it were to end. That was unimaginable, considering my childhood background. I had already made my decision. To have a child, I had to make two significant sacrifices: forfeiting my body and masculinity.

When I said yes to the challenges of the IVF process and procedures, I did not anticipate the physical, emotional, psychological, and financial tolls. The IVF cycle took months of planning, endless blood draws, and daily self-administered hormonal shots. It was a drawn out and stressful process.

Our first IVF attempt failed. I was devastated. Statistically, it was nearly impossible to have a child at my age. Then the fertility clinic offered an alternative option. They could request an egg donor, just like our sperm donor. At the end of another vigorous round of IVF, they implanted two growing embryos into my uterus. The odds of me getting pregnant as a surrogate mother nearly doubled.

Seven days post-IVF implant, I had my first blood draw to check my human chorionic gonadotropin (HCG) hormone level. If my HCG count was higher than zero, I was pregnant. My HCG count was at a seven! When I heard the news, my knees grew weak and I felt light-headed. *Oh my gosh. I am pregnant at the age of forty.* Jamie and I were going to have a baby.

Gay Christian Identity

In my heart, I saw my miraculous pregnancy as confirmation that I was on the right path and God was once again on my side. I was happily married and God was blessing us with the beginnings of a family. After years of searching and waiting, I finally had everything my heart desired. This was proof that salvation was available for affirmed gay Christians and that there was hope in a gay Christian identity.

I could not imagine my life any different or any better than this, but little could prepare me for what was ahead.

PART II

A RESURRECTED IDENTITY

9

NEW BIRTH

Flesh gives birth to flesh, but the Spirit gives birth to spirit.
Jesus (John 3:6)

Where the Wind Blows

The wind blows wherever it pleases. You hear its sound, but you
cannot tell where it comes from or where it is going. So, it is with
everyone born of the Spirit.
Jesus (John 3:8)

Our big day arrived! After mentally, physically, and emotionally preparing for the past nine months, it was time to bring our baby girl into the world. Enduring restless nights from chronic backaches, calf muscle cramps, and tiny happy feet dancing against my rib cage, I was ready to cross the finish line. I kept daydreaming about nights of continuous sleep once the baby arrived. I had no idea how absurd it was to think I would get more sleep after bringing home a newborn.

We really could not help ourselves from arriving at the hospital a half-hour early. We were too anxious and excited to sit around the house, waiting for the scheduled time. Our early arrival paid off because the nurses wasted no time in getting me checked in, prepped, and ready for action. Minutes before they induced labor, Jamie dared to ask the question, "Are you nervous?" I boastfully said, "Hey, if prissy heterosexual women can do this thing, then so can I!" About thirty minutes later, after the connected monitor captured an image outlining Alaska's highest mountain range, I reneged on my cocky attitude. Trying to overcome the excruciating pain, I pointed to the scenic view and murmured, "Hey, Doc, are these contractions going to get any higher?" She politely replied with a slight giggle, "No. They are pretty much maxed out." I failed to ask the most obvious question, "How long will these mega-contractions last?"

Five hours from the minute of induction, our daughter was born. At last, at the end of the race, I held my great reward—my precious little girl. It was love at first sight! As I touched her soft, sweet face and embraced her tiny body, I was in awe of the miracle of life. These indescribable feelings of joy and love superseded my physical exhaustion and pain. Yearning for a child conquers all things, including physical and emotional pain. Holding this living miracle made every financial, physical, and loving sacrifice worth it.

The hospital's delivery ward was several floors above the nursery, so we needed to move our celebration to our assigned hospital room. As one of the nurses wheeled my daughter and me through the elevator doors, another nurse standing at the back of the platform glanced at my swaddled bundle resting in my arms and said, "You have something special there." Glowing with pride, I immediately responded, "Yes, I do!" I had no idea yet that she was an out-of-the-ordinary child for extraordinary reasons.

In the seconds it took the elevator to descend four floors, I encountered the presence of the Holy Spirit and engaged in a spiritual conversation. The Holy Spirit, who is also known as the Spirit of Truth (John 15:26), unveiled my eyes to three profound truths concerning my spiritual life and the life of my newborn child.

Truth #1 – God Really Does Love Me!

As I stared down at the sweet face of my newborn, I felt the overwhelming presence of God's love embracing me like a child. The feeling of love was unfathomable and unconditional. As sure as nothing could separate my love from my daughter, I knew nothing could separate me from God's love. Shockingly, His pure love was without a trace of judgment or condemnation. This perfect love, in the purest form, reflected only the face and heart of God. Even though I did not deserve an ounce of His unfailing love, He was offering it to me freely. In all of my life, I had never felt such unconditional and immeasurable love. Even though I could not comprehend or fully accept it, I knew God truly loved me.

Truth #2 – My Child Is God's Child

It was God, and God alone, who had blessed me with this unique gift—my child (Psalm 127:3). This truth coincided with the first revelatory truth. God gifted me with a child out of His love and His salvation plan, and I did not deserve or earn any of it. Throughout my life, I had operated from the belief system that I was fully in charge of my destiny. I believed all rewards came from a person's strong will, self-control, and persistent determination, and that this child was a result of my true grit, along with the skills and expertise of the fertility physicians. Attempting to get pregnant at age forty was more about risky percentages and a costly financial gamble than a sovereign act of God. I had it all wrong. The conception and birth of this child was a perfect gift from the Maker of the heavens and earth who had a divine purpose. While judgmental Christians viewed this child as a symbol of abominable and wretched sin, God used this child as a ray of His Light. The same God who I once believed had forsaken me as a child was now entrusting me with His most precious gift of life—His child.

Truth #3 – I Am Living Against God

The Holy Spirit that comes and goes like the wind delivers what He is known for—conviction, not condemnation. The Spirit's voice cut through my heart with a soul-piercing question. Now awakened to the divine knowledge that God was with me, for me, and loves me, was my way of living going against this loving and gracious God?

The revelatory question left me dumbfounded. Who was I living for and trying to please—me, Jamie, or God? More disconcerting thoughts rushed through my mind's broken levy. Was my way of life genuinely acceptable and pleasing to God? Was this the way God wanted me to live and raise my child? As mysterious as the wind, doubts about my self-proclaimed redemption penetrated my soul.

As the elevator bell dinged and the doors opened to the floor of the hospital's nursery, I reentered my world. My conversation with God abruptly ended with my life's present reality. I was not in the condition nor state of mind to confront such difficult and consequential questions. Depending on the answers, there could be detrimental consequences. If I was living against God, how could I remove the noose around my neck without accidentally hanging myself? To radically change my way of life now would destroy the lives of partner and my child.

The effects of this spiritual experience kept cascading through my mind and heart. The idea of becoming a single mother terrified me. I felt I would fail her.

My spiritual enlightenment also threatened my relationship with Jamie because she did not believe in the same kind of god as me. Until this moment, our religious differences were never an issue for us. Jamie's agnostic faith became a real threat to what I believed God wanted for our daughter and myself. These were monumental hurdles I would have to overcome, one way or another.

To mentally cope, I had to keep pushing out these binding thoughts and keep myself grounded in realism.

Regardless of the uprising tension, it was a prodigious day. As our daughter took the first breath of her natural life, I took my first breath of a regenerated life.

The Tension

For the flesh desires what is contrary to the Spirit, and the Spirit, what is contrary to the flesh. They are in conflict with each other so that you are not to do whatever you want.
Galatians 5:17

Having a newborn in your home is quite the challenge, especially if it is your first child. I know every parent, regardless of gender, can relate to the stresses and nuances of being first-time parents. New mothers can suffer from a unique mental and physical condition called postpartum depression. My doctor warned us to watch for potential signs. Some common symptoms of postpartum depression are feelings of paranoia, hypervigilance, severe emotional distress, irritability, nightmares, trouble sleeping, etc. I cannot say for sure if I was suffering from postpartum depression, but I can confess that my first few weeks of motherhood were a problematic struggle, physically, emotionally, and mentally.

As a mother, I carried a unique burden. After struggling for so many years with my identity as a woman, I wondered if I had any maternal instincts. As a child, it was the identity and role of the mother I rejected. Initially, I felt like a fish out of water. I feared that my maternal incompetence would put my daughter's life in danger. A baby's cry always sent me into a nervous tizzy. What kept me leaning in and pushing forward in this role was my relentless love for my daughter. I started reading books to educate myself on how to take care of a baby. Falling in love with this child helped me fall in love with being a mother. For the first time in my life, I wanted to be a woman. My child unexpectedly helped me embrace my femininity and gender identity.

With each new day, motherhood became what it should be…joyful. As our child grew and reached her developmental milestones, I thrived at being a genuine, good mother, and cherished every second of it. I loved my newly inherited title—Mom.

When our daughter reached five months in age, our pastor confronted us about baptizing our daughter. Not having a background in the theology of the Presbyterian faith, or any religious denomination for that matter, I was not quite sure of the meaning behind a child's baptism. The thought of my daughter's baptism was more than intriguing; it was mysteriously compelling.

I made an appointment for us to meet and discuss our church's meaning of a child's baptism. When our pastor finished her explanation of the purpose of a child's baptism, it was an "aha" moment. A child's baptismal ceremony is a public declaration by the parents to vow to God their commitment to raise and develop their child's spiritual life. Before our congregation and God, we were to proclaim this lifelong commitment.

I was confident that our child's baptism was my next step. It was my first action in response to the Holy Spirit's truth revealed on my daughter's first day of life. It was my heart's desire to ensure our daughter knew and remembered where she came from and whom she belonged to. This decision to baptize her felt nonnegotiable and inevitable. God was already drawing my heart closer to Him.

To move forward with the baptism, our pastor informed us that we needed to have a spiritual witness who could hold us accountable to our promise to God. Only Tiffany came to mind. Since she was my biological sister and a Christian who would understand this act of commitment, she was the most logical choice. After extending my invitation, Tiffany accepted her role, and we set a date.

What I did not realize was that Tiffany had already invested in my daughter's spiritual life. Tiffany, along with members from her faith-based life group, including her oldest daughter's mother-in-law, Susan, had been praying for me for years. Susan knew me from my junior and senior years of high school when I was one of her student volunteers who assisted with her learning-disabled students. It was these two women and others who were praying continuously for my child and me. It was no coincidence that Tiffany was the appointed spiritual witness to our daughter's baptism. God had a higher plan in mind.

The significance of our daughter's baptism went beyond a public declaration. It signified a primal shift in the loyalty and desires of my heart. I wanted my daughter to know God. Choosing this path despite Jamie's disbelief of God marked a spiritual turning point in my life. It was my first step back to God. I was putting God before Jamie, and that had never happened before. She was my number one over everyone and everything, including my family, friends, and my wants and needs. My heart orientation was changing and turning in a different direction.

The balance of love between my daughter, God, and Jamie teetered. My love for my child drew me nearer to God and further away from anyone that opposed it. Jamie's lack of faith and indifference toward God started to become an obstacle in the direction I wanted to go with our daughter. Her hardened heart firmly opposed everything I felt God was calling me to, and the one area I refused to negotiate was the spiritual life of our daughter. The tension between Jamie and me escalated.

My spiritual life was also in the balance. I continued to deny that I was a sinner, and believed that the practice of homosexuality in a loving, monogamous relationship was not indwelling sin. What would be sin was to break my vow of marriage to Jamie. I had vowed to remain loyal to her for my entire life. Which would please God most? Breaking my marital promise or keeping it? Besides, since God had granted me a family, I had to protect it. If I failed with my same-sex marriage, abandoned Jamie, and destroyed my family, that would be a greater sin than any sexual immorality. God would surely not approve of a divorce. With all of my reasoning, I was still determined to fight for my marriage.

Over the next two years, there was an all-out spiritual battle over my family and me, and our daughter was in the crux of it. Regardless of my rationalizations, I could not shake the unveiled convictions given on the day my daughter was born. How could I possibly teach my daughter about Jesus Christ when I did not know Him? If I did not know Jesus, what did that mean about my salvation? This relentless tug-of-war amongst me, Jamie, and our daughter had to come to an end. I was wearily losing the battle.

My first reaction to this struggle was to fight harder for my idols, starting with my same-sex relationship. I wanted to fix our failing marriage, and my first dire approach was to chase after material things. We went on a rampage of purchases, such as new cars, new homes, and recreational vehicles. The dream that captivated our attention and kept us connected was our plans of a dreamy retreat home nestled in the foothills of the mountainous Northwest. We had already invested in four-plus acres only minutes away from a newly built top-class ski resort. We had inadvertently become owners of prime real estate that had quadrupled in value. Despite the monetary value of the land, it still was not enough to save us.

As a last-ditch effort, I wanted us to get professional help. Counseling had helped me out of the pits before, so maybe it could fix my marriage. I believed our marital issues had nothing to do with sin or God, but rather the typical marital problems. Our lives seemed to be in constant flux. We were dealing with new jobs and changed addresses, as well as becoming parents. Our differences in religion and faith mattered, too. We were facing rather significant obstacles, but surely nothing that professional counseling could not resolve.

We only attended a few therapy sessions before the counselor released us. However, she did not release us because of our earth-shattering breakthroughs but rather our impasses. Our relationship was at the point of no return. Our partnership gravely lacked mutual respect and healthy communication, which was a recipe for failure in any intimate relationship.

I had to make a choice.

Awakened Identity

Very truly I tell you, no one can enter the kingdom of God
unless they are born of water and the Spirit.
Jesus (John 3:5)

This sudden onset of inner tension between my spirit and the Holy Spirit was undeniably real. By the work of the Holy Spirit aligning with God's perfect plan and impeccable timing, God chose to breathe spiritual life into my soul as my daughter inhaled her first breath of life.

My spiritual birth brought three great truths I could no longer deny or escape. God loves me regardless of my love for Him, my child was His child, and my way of living went against His way.

My awakened identity was a gift by a loving and gracious God, yet the question remained. What was I going to do about it?

10

COMING HOME

We had to celebrate this happy day.
For your brother was dead and has come back to life!
He was lost, but now he is found!
Luke 15:32 (NLT)

Letting Go

Trust in the Lord with all your heart and lean not on your own
understanding; in all your ways submit to him,
and he will make your paths straight.
Proverb 3:5-6

Letting go hurts, even if it is for a good reason. It is always scary at first too.

Despite our efforts to save it, my same-sex partnership crumbled, and my life came crashing down. We forfeited our promises for our differences.

Since our separation occurred long before the United States had legalized same-sex marriage, our relationship covenant was not legal by state law. We had to make all our difficult decisions without any fair arbitration. A same-sex break-up is as devastating as any heterosexual divorce, but we were fighting this out on our own.

As a child, I had witnessed several violent acts and tantrums thrown by my biological father and J.W. Now, I found myself close to crossing that same line.

Our last fight erupted during our daughter's evening bath. We both lost our temper and were lashing out at each other. What halted the fight was the hysterical cry of our child. Our heated altercation petrified her. She had never seen us fight like this. Our battle tactics were more passive-aggressive, such as stonewalled conversations, disrespectful glares, and negative, nonverbal body language. This fight was dangerously different. The look of terror on her face took my breath away. How could I have let it come to this? My life was spinning out of control.

Invite from Heaven

Come to me, all who are weary and burdened,
and I will give you rest.
Jesus (Matthew 11:28)

In defeat, I retreated to my place of shame: our home's guest bedroom. As I laid on the bed sobbing, my emotions were in a tailspin. How was I going to get out of this mess with any sanity or integrity? My failures were now impacting another innocent life. I was dragging my child through the gates of hell.

My darkest moment was when I realized I could no longer trust myself. Not one part of me: my beliefs, my feelings, or my heart. After all, it was my heart that had led me into this mess. Where did I go now? I was at the end of myself, and I felt like a complete failure. What made this so excruciating was knowing my daughter was paying for my mistakes.

The thought of living as a single parent terrified me. Was I strong enough to survive on my own? Money was always a worry. Leaving meant I would be raising a child on a single income. Fear owned me, and I kept procrastinating. I knew that once I moved out, there was no turning back.

In desperation, I cried out to the one who was for me—God.

God, I am in a mess I do not know how to get out of. I have destroyed three lives, and I do not know where to turn. I can no longer do this on my own.

Karol, Come Home

As I lay there alone on the bed in complete darkness, I heard a soft and gentle voice whisper, "Karol, come home." Although I did not recognize His voice, I am confident today that it was the voice of Jesus. It is Jesus who leaves his flock of ninety-nine to find the one (Matthew 18:12-13). It is God's sovereign plan that Jesus fulfills (John 6:44). It is Jesus who laid down his life to save a friend (John 15:13), and God knew I needed a friend to rescue me.

I instinctively knew what coming home required. It was the haunting truth I had been struggling with since I encountered the Holy Spirit on the day my daughter was born. If I accepted Jesus' invitation, it would require a courageous step in faith that would cost me everything. At this point, though, I had already lost everything. My same-sex relationship, my home, my way of life, and my gay-identified redemption. To return home to God's kingdom, I had to pack up, literally, and move out from my fallen empire.

The gripping thought of leaving behind all that I had ever known and believed was petrifying. What would I live for? Yet, Jesus' invitation offered me something I had always wanted: an invitation to a place where someone knows me and still wants me. I was tired of running away from my problems. I was exhausted from proving my worthiness and defending my earned redemption. After years of chasing conditional love, my restless heart was once again homeless. To have Jesus, who sits at the right hand of God, call me out by name, and extend a way out of my self-dug grave, won me over. This orphan child could not resist this personal and compelling invitation—a way back to an enduring place owned by a loving God who truly wanted me in His home.

Turning Back

Answer me, Lord, answer me, so these people will know that you,
Lord, are God, and that you are turning their hearts back again.
1 Kings 18:37

The next morning, I woke with greater strength and courage. I could not explain where I was getting this renewed power, because my self-power was running on empty. Today, I do not doubt that this new kind of inner strength comes only from the heavens above. I clearly heard the voice of Jesus calling me home, and I was ready to go.

I had to let go of the fight and get myself and my daughter out of that self-defeating environment as quickly as possible. To leave so suddenly meant I was putting myself at risk of losing everything I rightfully owned. I knew the move could be a costly sacrifice, but I was determined to go in the direction God was taking me.

By 9:00 a.m., I was on the phone calling every apartment leasing office. I was looking for any short-term, month-by-month leasing options, regardless of the cost. By the end of the day, I had placed a deposit on a decent two-bedroom apartment located only a few miles from work. The place was perfect for us. By Saturday evening, with only clothes and a few essentials, my daughter and I moved into our new place. I was ready for a fresh start.

By choosing to take our daughter with me, I had to make serious decisions. I needed to find another preschool for my daughter. Jamie and I had taken advantage of her employer's daycare plan, and our daughter had gone there since she was only three months old. Now that we were separating for good, everything had to change. The preschool I was seeking gave more insight into my radical heart change. It was the utmost priority my daughter attend a Christian preschool. I knew I needed a lot of assistance to teach her about God. Since it was September, all preschool attendances were completely booked for the entire school year. It was going to be nearly impossible to find an opening at any preschool at this time of the year, much less a Christian preschool.

I could hardly believe it when I saw a Christian preschool located on my new route to work from my new apartment. I called immediately. Initially, they told me they did not have any openings for two-to-three-year-old toddlers. In desperation, I pleaded my case and explained my circumstances of being a newly single parent and wanting my child not only to learn but to also learn as much as possible about God. Later that day, the director of the school called me and presented the improvised option to place my daughter in her three-to-four-year-old classroom, assuming she could adjust. I was ecstatic. I knew this had to be the work of God. He was clearing the path and opening every door along the way.

Each day that I spent as a single parent, I was gaining new strength and confidence with my decisions and single parenthood. To my daughter, our move was an adventure. To me, it was a stressful nightmare. It was a drastic change in our way of life. I missed living in a home, and I had to keep reminding myself that this was only temporary. Someday, we would have a home again.

To the world around me, my heart change toward God seemed invisible. My close friend, Sophie, who had known me for the past seven years, walked alongside me through the entire break-up. The failure of my same-sex partnership came as no surprise to her since she witnessed the fallout. She knew this ending was inevitable. When I called and asked for her help to move us out of my house, it was not a surprise. What did catch her off guard were my reasons for wanting to move...and so quickly. I kept talking passionately about God and sharing that He was behind all of this. My friend's covert response was, "Yeah, right." She knew me well, and she knew that this was not my usual behavior. To her, there was only one logical explanation. I had to be running away from my problems. My religious chatter seemed foolish. She was right about one thing. I was running, but not away from my crisis—I was running to God.

There was another unusual character change that took place: my heart attitude toward Christianity. I began tuning in and listening to Christian music. The one song that captured my heart was "Jesus, Take the Wheel" by Carrie Underwood.

Carrie's song depicted my life at the moment. The lyrics uncannily spoke to my heart's desire and to what God was calling me to. It was such an inspiring song because it helped me see that I needed to let go and let Jesus. Like the song, I had a child strapped in the back seat of my truck and I desperately needed Jesus to take the wheel. Every time I heard the song play, I could feel my spirit yielding to God. My now two-year-old daughter loved the song, too. For the longest time, it was our number one jam whenever we took to the road.

Child custody is the most challenging and heart-wrenching aspect of a divorce, and my divorce was no different. Jamie had already decided to move closer to her family, and I felt compelled to move closer to mine. Our diverging desires pointed us to different destinations, making it nearly impossible to share custody of our child. It was unimaginable to accept, but I eerily found myself in the same place as my parents. One parent was going to have to abandon their child. I struggled with this tension for days, weeks, and months, but nothing could bring me to leave my child. I would rather die than forfeit a single parental right. Jamie made her own choices. After she chose her path, it made it simpler for me to choose mine. She was the first to move. From that point on, we were living two different lives in two different places, going in two different directions, and following two different gods.

I was not about to abandon my daughter's spiritual life. She was God's child, and I knew God had appointed me to nurture her spiritual growth. To deliver this promise, I had only one choice. To keep pursuing God, I needed to completely break away from Jamie and raise our daughter on my own. Once I made that decision, I never looked back.

Without a doubt, God was calling me back to my roots. I needed to be closer to my family, who were all living in the Midwest. I wanted to relocate to Kansas City. It was an excellent central location for all my immediate family, and a safe and affordable place to raise a child.

Despite my relentless efforts to find a job in Kansas City, the door seemed locked. I could not figure out why God was taking his time unlocking this door when all other doors had opened in perfect timing.

Then came my one and only job lead. I had applied for an Information Technology Application Analyst position for a large corporation in the outskirts of Kansas City, Kansas. My first interview was a phone interview with the hiring manager. I scheduled it during my lunch hour so I could talk privately from within my car and not have to worry about work interruptions. I did not want anything to blow this opportunity.

I was so surprised at how easy this manager was to talk to. Based on what he was looking for, I felt confident that I was qualified. However, the outstanding question was timing. I lived 1,400 miles away from the jobsite, and he wanted to hire someone in the next two weeks. Then he made an unbelievable offer. To get this job, all I had to do was show up Monday morning by 9:00 a.m. At first, I thought he was joking, but he was completely serious. I immediately accepted his offer. I had my airline tickets purchased by the end of my lunch hour. Job interviews with large corporations like that are never that easy, and again, this had to be God.

I surprised our family by flying in on the weekend before my scheduled appointment. In just two days, I scouted out apartments and Christian preschools located near the jobsite. If this manager offered me the job, I was going to have to act fast. By Sunday night, I knew where I wanted to live and what preschool my daughter would attend.

As soon as I entered the manager's office and shook his hand, the job was mine. It was the craziest thing I had ever experienced in the twenty-plus years of my professional career. He offered me the position, agreed to a salary, and gave me three weeks until my start date. I returned to Idaho with a long checklist of things to do in a matter of days. Although I was leaving behind good friends, a great job, and a beautiful place to live, I was confident in where God was taking me.

The Response

Everyone who drinks this water will be thirsty again,
but whoever drinks the water I give them will never thirst.
Jesus (John 4:13)

Three weeks later, we arrived at our leased apartment in the suburbs of Kansas City, Kansas…on Mother's Day. I could not think of a better way of launching our new life.

It was such a blessing to be near family. It had been nineteen years since I lived close to my family. I was delighted for my daughter to finally know her grandparents, aunts, uncles, and cousins, and I humbly welcomed their support.

The excitement of my new beginning overcame the anxiety that naturally comes with significant life changes. My daughter quickly acclimated to her teachers and classmates, which put me at ease. I smoothly transitioned into my new job. As I reminisced on my life changes over the past three years, I could see God's loving hand guiding us, protecting us, and providing our needs with impeccable timing. I had done everything God had asked of me up to this point, and He had delivered us.

Just a few weeks into my new life in Kansas City, as I was peacefully worshipping God with K-LOVE during my morning commute, I had an overwhelming sense to talk with God. I could feel the words coming out of my heart and hanging off the tip of my tongue. I really did not know how to pray to God, but in this exact moment, none of that really seemed to matter. I knew I was finally ready to let go of what I was holding back. It was time to release this indwelling spiritual tension, once and for all. I opened my mouth and out came words of wholehearted repentance:

God, I know you have been waiting for this moment for a long time. I have given you my daughter's physical and spiritual life as you so desired, but I have not given you the last thing—me. I am ready to provide you with what you have always wanted—all of me. I promise to leave behind my homosexual life permanently. I am DONE with that life. I know how you cherish the covenant between a man and a woman because marriage is your design. So, I am vowing to you like a bride to her groom. I promise to be faithful to you for the rest of my life, as a wife is to her husband. I am saying yes. No matter what temptations I may face, I will always remain faithful. If that means I have to lock myself up in a closet to conquer temptation, I will.

God, I have rebelliously sinned against you for thirty years, and I have made a mess of my life and the lives of others. I am so tired of smashing my life into concrete walls, and I no longer want to be in the driver's seat. Lord, please take the wheel. I am done driving.

As soon as the word *amen* passed through my lips, I felt the chains drop. My body actually felt lighter. I had no idea that my rebellious, indwelling sin was not only death to my spirit but also a heavy burden on my physical body. Jesus released my shackled chains, and, in June 2007, after nearly a thirty-year wrestle with my homosexuality, I was set free (John 8:32)!

I felt nothing but pure, spontaneous, immeasurable joy and peace flowing in and through my soul. If a theologian were to tell me that a person's moment of spiritual conversion takes place in the heavenly realm as well as the earthly, I would believe it wholeheartedly.

As I reflected on the oath I had just made to God, I chuckled aloud. How ironic was that? After living a decade as a closeted lesbian, I was willing to go back into the closet if that was what it took to be faithful and obedient to God. Since I am His creation, God must have a sense of humor.

Chosen Identity

Before I formed you in the womb, I knew you,
before you were born, I set you apart.
Jeremiah 1:4-5

Little did I know how long God had actually waited for this moment. After thirty years of rejecting and displeasing Him, He never gave up on me. From my conception, He relentlessly pursued me. It is God's will and desire for *no one* to perish (Hebrews 4:11). Only a merciful and forgiving God would freely give me a chosen identity when I least expected it.

11

BORN FROM ABOVE

To all who believed in Jesus and accepted him, he gave the right to
become children of God. They are reborn—not with a physical birth
resulting from human passion or plan, but a birth that comes from God.
John 1:12-13

From the moment I vowed to God to sacrifice my life and faithfully follow His ways, I have continued to experience supernatural transformation. In the thirteen years since, some of my transformational experiences have been instantaneous, while others have been slow and progressive over a period of time...sometimes years. Regardless of the timing, I can positively say that I am not the same person I was in my pre-Jesus era. This spiritual metamorphosis started in the depths of my soul, beginning with a renewed mind, a new body image, and a radically changed heart. This new spiritual journey with Jesus has given me a whole new respect and understanding of the words *born again*.

Only God can make something possible out of the impossible. My changes had nothing to do with my willpower, ethical behavior, or striving, but everything to do with the identity of the Trinity: God's plan, Jesus' sacrificial price, and the Holy Spirit's power. The only responsibility I can claim is the cyclical actions of surrender, repentance, and obedience to what the Holy Spirit convicted me of.

Until I fully recognized and allowed God to forgive my sins, nothing would happen. I would have snuck through the pearly gates of heaven on Judgment Day, but I would have left every single heavenly reward unclaimed. I knew that I must always be willing to humbly admit and repent of my sins and continuously obey Jesus out of love if I expected the Holy Spirit to do His transformative work inside of me. I knew I had to uproot sin and invite obedience in all aspects of my life. All this change is impossible by man, but entirely possible with God (Mark 10:27).

Renewed Mind

Throw off your old sinful nature and your former way of life, which is
corrupted by lust and deception. Instead, let the Spirit renew your
thoughts and attitudes. Put on your new nature, created to be like
God—truly righteous and holy.
Ephesians 4:22-24 (NLT)

The first distinguishable and instantaneous transformation happened in the attitude of my mind. My thoughts were radically turned around from my old way of thinking to a fundamentally new way of thinking, and it came as a surprise.

God did an extraordinary U-turn with my thoughts about women. He rescued and delivered me from past decades of dealing with deeply rooted same-sex feelings and sexual attractions by eliminating the roots of desire. Instead of *out of sight equaled out of mind,* it was vice versa. Out of mind equaled out of sight. When I looked at beautiful women, even my eyes were faithful to God. I no longer fantasized or lusted over other women's looks, personalities, or bodies. The renewal of my mind was the first sign of conversion.

Although I believe this was an instantaneous change, it took a while for me to trust in new thought patterns and heart attitudes toward women. I kept looking for intellectual and psychological reasons for this mind shift. Like most doubters, I went through a list of human possibilities.

At first, I pointed to stress. Over three consecutive years, I gave birth to a child at age forty-one, went through a devastating break-up, moved over five times between two states over a thousand miles apart, and changed jobs, all while parenting a toddler as a single parent. Over many days and months, I felt overwhelmed by the inundating feelings and thoughts of failing. My coping mechanism was to emotionally shut down. Maybe, my uncompromising stress and physical exhaustion were suppressing my same-sex attraction. Even after the pressure declined, though, my mind still held a stronghold on sexual purity and holiness.

Maybe it was just a season I was going through, and once I got my life settled and in order, I would once again struggle with the temptations of same-sex attraction. Perhaps I was in a dormant season, like perennial plants in the dark and cold winter months. When I came out of hibernation, I would have to control my ravishing hunger pangs. When that happened, it would be only a matter of time before I would have to once again claw my way out of my old sexual nature and temptations. Seasons came and went, though, and still my mind stayed loyal to God.

When my thoughts and eyes no longer caused me to stumble, I knew God had done something remarkable. As I continued to bump into attractive women, including lesbians, I felt an insurmountable love, *without want*. Imagine the immense joy and peace that comes from someone conquering cancer, or overcoming a lifetime addiction, or being resuscitated back to life after near death. This is how I felt about my newfound freedom from sexual sin. To have a pure mind, consecrated eyes, and transparent motives toward women is indeed an indescribable gift.

The other compelling evidence of this mind makeover was the sustaining power to never return to my previous ways. If I ever do find myself struggling with sexual temptation again, I am confident that I would not return to my old self. Once I discovered and unburied this heaven-sent treasure, I would sell everything to hang on to it. It is just like the way Jesus describes it in Matthew 13:44, "The Kingdom of Heaven is like a treasure that a man discovered hidden in a field. In his excitement, he hid it again and sold everything he owned to get enough money to buy the field." After stumbling upon the treasures of this kind of freedom delivered by the love of Jesus Christ, I bought in.

For the first time ever, I wanted to look, feel, and act like a woman. I was ready to unmask my femininity and let go of my long-held masculinity. To honor and please God for the way He had created me from the womb, I wanted to be a woman of God. To do that, I wanted to embrace the gender I was born with.

The expression of femininity and masculinity are not for us to judge or stereotype. However, learning to embrace and respect my biological sex and female gender identity were pure expressions of my intimate praise to my Creator.

Blossoming into femininity was not an overnight success. It would take over a decade to undergo this transformation. My first inclination was to change my hairstyle. I know that there are many sassy and sexy short hairstyles worn by feminine women, but for me, my short hairstyle was an intentional choice that once identified my struggling gender identity. Thanks to my patient and incredibly talented hairstylist, Nathan, I am confident in my new, long hair. My hair is now a constant and symbolic reminder of my gender restoration, all done by the hands of God.

There was also the surmountable challenge of comfortably wearing women's apparel. As I sometimes would cut through the men's clothing department, it felt surreal. Like a faint dream, I could no longer remember the details or feelings as to why I wanted to wear men's clothing. It was like that part of my brain was no longer there. Although I was relieved that I had no desire for men's apparel, entering the women's clothing department still felt foreign and awkward. I was overwhelmed with the absurd number of styles and accessories to choose from. When I finally did see something I liked, I still did not have the confidence to wear it. Initially, I had to go shopping with close friends and family to help me learn what looked fitting and appropriate. I was like a teenage girl all over again.

While shopping and fashion were second nature to other women, they became victorious milestones for me. I now know why women take hours to shop. The sheer volume of stores, styles, sizes, and brands to choose from is astronomical!

I am finally now confident and comfortable wearing simple dresses and skirts. I love my manicures and pedicures. I still do have limitations, like wearing three- to four-inch heels, which is due more to safety and comfort concerns, rather than fashion statements. I still hate shopping, but I do like wearing women's clothes, make-up, and showing off my long hair. I can boastfully say that Jesus gave me victory over my gender identity as well as breaking down barriers of an insecure body image.

Though lustful sin no longer enslaved my mind, not all aspects of my mental health were perfect and sinless. I still had to learn how to establish healthy, emotional boundaries with other women, straight or gay. Early in my spiritual journey, on two separate occasions, I had become emotionally close and connected to two women who were both wives and mothers. At first, I was perplexed and scared as to why I enjoyed these women's company so much. I started to doubt my freedom of same-sex feelings, as the enemy wanted me to. Then I realized, with the help of one of my spiritual mentors, what was drawing me to these women. It was their nurturing and encouraging personalities. What I was longing for was a deeper relational connection. That is completely normal for every human being.

God created us as relational beings. Establishing intimacy with others is expected. What we often interfuse is intimacy with sex. Intimate relationships with other human beings can and should exist outside of sexual relations. It is God's given desire for me to be connected and close with other people without crossing unhealthy emotional and sexual boundaries. I still have more to learn about establishing and navigating healthy boundaries and relationships with women, but I am so grateful for how far I have come.

Then there was my attitude shift toward men. My initial problem with men was not necessarily in the department of physical attraction. I respected and appreciated handsome men almost as much as straight women. My issues with men went deeper into my heart attitude. All through my homosexual life, I deeply resented men for having everything that I wanted. It took a while for me to see that I was still holding onto this resentment for no apparent reason.

As I began to unpack these feelings, I started seeing a common theme. I did not know how to relate to men from a woman's perspective. Men were always my peers, not my pursuit. Feeling emotionally connected and physically submissive to men felt frightening and vulnerable. There was a locked door that stood in between me and my feelings toward men, and I did not possess the key.

It was not until I went on a family mission trip a few years ago, where I ministered alongside men of God, that I felt convicted of my hardened heart. One night, while I laid in bed, praying about that day's events, I broke down in tears when God revealed the real character of these godly men that I had been judging for decades. Following the conviction, I immediately repented.

The next morning, I confessed to each man on our team and asked for their forgiveness. From then on, I welcomed all men as my true brothers in Jesus Christ.

Renewed Sexuality

God's will is for you to be holy, so stay away from all sexual sin.
Then each of you will control his own body and live in holiness and
honor—not in lustful passion like the pagans
who do not know God and his ways.
1 Thessalonians 4:3-5 (NLT)

When it came to my renewed sexuality, I expected the least and braced for the worst. After promising sexual faithfulness to God, I knew I had to resign to a life of celibacy. That seemed like another impasse that I could not achieve on my own. The odds of a middle-aged lesbian becoming emotionally connected to men were as good as winning the lottery. I was just going to have to anchor down and painfully endure a barren life without the luxury of sex.

The worldly perspective was often that no sane person could survive life without sex, at least joyfully. I believed this lie. I felt that for me to live as a celibate, loyal servant meant that I had to forfeit a fulfilling life in exchange for my eternal salvation. My sexuality, regardless of its redefined orientation, would have to be placed upon the altar as a daily sacrifice. Very few churches and Christians ever talked about celibacy as a viable and fulfilling pathway for single people. The primary takeaway I got from church was that singleness was a transitory state until we found that one right person to marry. Singleness was not to be advertised as this life choice or an anointing pathway unless I wanted to become a Catholic nun. My assumption was that there was no such thing as sustaining joy for single, celibate people.

What I underestimated was the indwelling power that lived in one celibate person—Jesus. Jesus warns us to tread lightly and faithfully on our path of sexuality in Matthew 19:11-12, where He addresses the concepts of marriage, divorce, and celibacy: "Not everyone can accept this statement, only those whom God helps. Some are born as eunuchs, some have been made eunuchs by others, and some choose not to marry for the sake of the Kingdom of Heaven. Let anyone accept this who can."

The first time I read this Scripture, I knew it was speaking of me. I can and have accepted my celibacy as God's will.

I am coming upon fourteen years as a genuinely content celibate Christian. I can testify that the joy, love, and peace I have experienced while living as a single person has far surpassed all past romantic relationships as a whole. Every Christian has access to the same indwelling power of the Holy Spirit to say no to all sexual temptation while joyfully sustaining sexual purity. In John 6:35 (NLT), when Jesus says, "I am the bread of life", that means He *is* enough. In the same verse, Jesus also says, "Whoever comes to me will never be hungry again. Whoever believes in me will never be thirsty." Because of Jesus, I no longer hunger and thirst for unhealthy cravings. When we live by the Spirit, we walk lighter by way of Jesus. If Jesus could sustain a celibate life, going against His society's majority, then so can I.

My faithfulness to God, has made me one with Jesus. "The person who is joined to the Lord is one spirit with him" (1 Corinthians 6:17). My intimacy needs have been, and always will be, fulfilled by the one and only Savior, Jesus. People often get tattoos of the names of people they love. The name of Jesus, in the Hebrew language, is tattooed on my right arm for this very reason. For now, He is the only man, in heaven and on earth, that has truly won my heart.

If God chooses marriage for me, then so be it. Either way, I am trusting God with my life and honoring Him with my body (1 Corinthians 6:20). I believe both celibacy and marriage between a man and woman are spiritual gifts given by God and according to His will. As Jesus says, "...I want your will to be done, not mine" (Luke 22:42b). These words not only apply to my walk of faith, but also to my sexuality.

Resurrected Heart

I will give you a new heart, and I will put a new spirit in you.
I will take out your stony, stubborn heart and give you
a tender, responsive heart.
Ezekiel 36:26

An awakened heart by the Holy Spirit generates a new kind of heartbeat. My resurrected heart went from hardened and cold to compassionate and fully alive.

My heart attitude toward God was another one of those crazy, instantaneous turnarounds. I went from being a timid person that spoke only a few words about my Christian faith to nonstop rambling about God's unfailing love, mercy, and sovereignty. Although I was afraid to share my history for fear of judgment, I no longer felt embarrassed to share what I believed about God with others. My heart turned immediately into an evangelistic heart. My compelling desire to share my love for God was inevitably the first sign of a newly regenerated spirit.

Then there was the constant and convicting heart tug to reconcile my past relationships with all of my immediate family members. I wish I could say I championed this command without errors or mistakes, but that was far from reality. I made a wreck of my family life by allowing years of resentment, anger, and judgment own me. Warming up this cold, stony heart took years. I had to walk out God's definition of mercy, grace, and forgiveness, without excuse or complaint, and that took nearly a decade for me to master—and I am still a work in progress.

> *Be completely humble and gentle; be patient, bearing with one*
> *another in love. Make every effort to keep the unity of the Spirit*
> *through the bond of peace.*
> *Ephesians 4:2-3*

Jesus is the Peacemaker. To follow in His ways, I needed to lay down my armor and weapons and make peace with my past. God had a much deeper purpose in my return to Kansas City, and I was starting to see it. God had not only put me in the heart of the U.S.A., but He placed me in the heart of my immediate family, geographically and emotionally.

The first place I was drawn to make peace was with my biological father, and for a good reason. Dad got to meet his granddaughter for the first time. That in itself brought healing, peace, and joy to both us. My daughter loved meeting her Grandpa Adams, and, undoubtedly, he loved her. Although Dad's mental health never recovered or improved, his mind was still lively and coherent within his decaying body. His favorite pastime was reminiscing our childhood days. I could tell by how he talked that Dad knew God personally, and on occasion, I could hear the words of remorse coming from his crackling voice. My last visit with Dad was shared alongside my sister Rachel and my daughter. We sat laughing and joking with him while he laid in his nursing home bed. Three weeks later, Dad passed away in his sleep on April 27, 2012. I thank God for this brief reunion with my father, whom I will always cherish as my long-ago childhood hero. I am looking forward to our final reunion, where I know Dad is saving a place for me.

The second relationship I needed to reconcile and restore was with my biological mother. I knew I was commanded to honor my father and mother, and the Spirit was not going to let up until I figured out how. The person I now lived in closest proximity to, yet avoided the most, was my biological mother. I had no excuse for my behavior except for my own stubbornness. I realized that I needed as much of the power of the Holy Spirit to forgive as I needed to be celibate. Once I realized that I had no rightful authority to judge or condemn people, I had to choose to walk in full forgiveness. My mother was no exception. If Jesus forgave me of my sin, then I had to forgive others, or I was not a follower of Jesus. It was that simple.

There was no one moment that I can point to that turned my heart around toward my mother. It was an incremental process filled with failures and repeated surrender. I am thankful to God for encouraging and leading me to a place of peace with my daughter's grandmother and step-grandfather. My daughter cherished every day she spent with Ooma and Poppy, as she called them. For me to say I wholeheartedly love and honor my mother and stepfather despite our rocky past is another powerful testament to the healing and reconciling love of Jesus. Again, God's timing was perfect because Poppy was diagnosed with esophageal cancer in early 2009 and died on October 18th. Jesus is the hope of reconciliation: between us and God our Father, and with each other (2 Corinthians 5:19).

For the last fourteen years, my daughter and I have thoroughly enjoyed reconnecting with my biological and adoptive family. When we first returned to Kansas City, my daughter called her family "my people". She had it so right. Whether by blood or spirit, those who believe in Jesus were our mothers, brothers, and sisters in Christ (Mark 3:35). They were our people.

My "resurrected heart" artwork, painted during my life's darkest moments nearly twenty-eight years ago, did capture my heart's transformation.. Little did I know then that I was painting a picture of my resurrected heart transformed by the love of God. I could not have chosen any other front cover for this book other than this prophetic image. After searching for unfailing love all of my life, I discovered it where I least expected it—in Jesus!

Born-Again Identity

Take off the grave clothes and let him [or her] go.
Jesus (John 11:44)

"Out of the grave" is the most exceptional description of a born-again believer. Jesus raised me from the dead with the same resurrected power from the Holy Spirit that raised Him from the dead (Ephesians 1:19-20). Like every born-again believer, through His transformational power, I am a modern-day miracle.

Spiritual rebirth is an act of our Almighty God. We are reborn children only by birth that comes from God, through the supernatural work of the Holy Spirit. By this power, I am now a temple of the Holy Spirit: "Do you not know that your bodies are temples of the Holy Spirit, who is in you, whom you have received from God? You are not your own" (1 Corinthians 6:19).

The simple truth was that I never could have changed any part of my nature on my own. Only by my faith in Jesus am I lifted and restored to His righteousness and holiness.

If Jesus raised Lazarus' dead body that was already buried for four days, then why would we doubt that Jesus has raised and transformed me?

12

A PLACE FOR ME

*To the church of God in Corinth, to those sanctified in Christ Jesus
and called to be his holy people, together with all those everywhere
who call on the name of our Lord Jesus Christ—their Lord and ours.*
1 Corinthians 1:2

Plugging In

After handing over my life, heart, identity, and feelings to God, I dared to ask the next question: "Now what do I do?" I was embarrassed to confess not knowing anything from His written word. Although I was eager to obey, I did not know what else God commanded of Christians.

God's next step came through immediately and clearly. He broke through my thoughts and replied with three simple words: "Get plugged in." I knew what God was asking me to do. He was telling me to find a church where I could join other believers, grow nearer to Him, and learn about Jesus.

Oh, heck no. Plugging myself into a church meant God was calling me to connect and integrate among other Christians. But this was my next step, whether I liked it or not. Purposely entering a church building filled with heterosexual Christians was the last thing I wanted to do. I had spent the last thirty years avoiding and hating these people. Now I was to join in fellowship with them? The thought of integrating with the people that rejected and condemned me felt far more impossible than resisting any same-sex temptations.

Then I thought about my kind, the LGBTQ community. What would they think about me joining the other side? To turn to God and His church was a clear delineation of betrayal. I knew the LGBTQ community would tag me as a traitor. I was quite experienced with the great divide between the LGBTQ community and Christians, and I had fought the battle wholeheartedly from the side of the LGBTQ. I knew I had a bullseye target on the front of me as well as my back.

Despite my feelings, God did not seem too concerned with my comfort level. God had one specific goal in mind—for me to know and become like His son Jesus and get connected with His people. Belonging to God's family of believers is as essential to a reborn spirit as a mother's breast milk is to an infant. My spiritual growth required immediate nourishment and God's indisputable next step steered me toward other brothers and sisters in Christ.

Every godly command depends on an act of obedience. My foremost obstacle to willful obedience was doubt. I highly questioned how I would find the right church in a large metropolitan city that I barely knew. There were hundreds of registered churches in the metro area of Kansas City, spanning multiple denominations. Joining a church family that welcomed me was as probable as finding a needle in a haystack. More importantly, what kind of church would accept and believe in a miraculous redeemed-lesbian testimony like mine? There was no way I could make all the right decisions without any in-depth knowledge of churches, their doctrines, and denominations. I had more impending doubts about God's ability to lead me to the right church than leading me to a holy sexuality.

God had me right where He wanted me. It was at the end of my own knowledge and understanding that I uncovered God's knowledge and wisdom. In contrast to my thinking, God was not expecting me to do any of this on my own. Instead, what He wanted was total reliance, wholehearted trust, and a willful spirit to obey whatever He called me to. Whenever God opened a door, it was my responsibility to act and step across the threshold in faith. This was my first lesson on the interlinking of faith and obedience.

Another life now relied on my obedience. Now that I was the head of the household, every choice I made had a direct impact on my daughter's well-being. Whichever church I chose, it had to nourish her spiritual needs as well as mine. I did not take this decision lightly. The good news was that my daughter's spiritual nourishment could come from other sources beyond a one-hour Sunday school class.

Upon the first day at her new Christian preschool, my daughter made a new best friend. It turned out that her new friend, Aspen, was also a newcomer to preschool, and each other's company brought comfort and connection. Every day, I got to hear all about her daily adventures with Aspen.

One day, while picking up my daughter after work, I ran into Aspen's mother, Phuc. Like our daughters, our chance encounter instantly changed us from acquaintances to friends. Phuc and her husband Dave were the most genuine and kind people. It came as no surprise to discover that they were loyal followers of Jesus. When they invited me to go to church with them, I knew it had to be God opening the door I needed to enter. I did not have to question the theology of their church because I instinctively trusted Dave and Phuc from the moment I met them. In encountering them, I was building faith and trust in God. He was behind every circumstance. Dave, Phuc, and sweet Aspen were sent by God for His soon-to-be revealed purpose.

Shortly after meeting Dave and Phuc, I felt compelled to share my story. It was a risky and bold move to tell them so early in our friendship without knowing how they would react to my homosexual past. The highest risk was losing them as friends, and the greatest fear was encountering disbelief and more condemnation. Once I put more profound thought into it, I had no choice but to open up and share. I knew it was disgraceful to God to bury the truth of this testimony out of fear. What good was it for God to form a new creation and then hide it in the dark? I needed to get over myself and trust God.

It went far better than I ever could have expected. Dave and Phuc wholeheartedly believed in my story. Phuc responded, "Karol, more Christians need to hear your story, and maybe someday, I will be reading about it." I distinctly remember laughing and thinking that would never happen. I had every intention to keep this story preserved for God and a select few people. Obviously, God had a different plan.

Then came the first Sunday morning that I promised to join Phuc and her family for church. Knowing that we had decided to drive separately and meet there eased some of my anxiousness. I kept telling myself that if I got too freaked out, I could leave on my own. I was sure that Dave and Phuc would not hold it against me if I decided to bolt. I believe they knew how difficult it was for me to trust Christians. They gave me all the space and time that I needed.

I was surprised and relieved to know that their church congregation was currently meeting at an elementary school. Large church buildings and big gatherings were intimidating, and I was already anxiously concerned about not fitting in. When I walked into the school's hallways, the atmosphere of this ordinary place was filled with light. Everyone had smiles on their faces and were intentionally greeting one another. I tried to avoid making contact because I knew if I looked them in the eyes, they would stop and introduce themselves. I was not yet ready for that. My mission was to quickly get my daughter checked into Sunday school and then make a dash to the dimly lit auditorium, where I could blend in.

Where I chose to sit in the auditorium was just as important. I did not want to be near the front of the stage where the light would expose me. I tried to find a row of empty seats in the darkest part of the room so no one would see me or sit on either side of me. Once I got settled in, I could finally relax as I listened to the worship songs coming from the band on stage.

As the gifted vocalists looked up to the heavens and raised their voices in songs of praise, my heart melted. As I listened to the lyrics, I started crying uncontrollably. The tears streaming down my face were not of sorrow or sadness, but of extreme joy and adoration. I could not wrap my brain around how much God loved me and the reasons why. After all the things I had done for so long, I could not comprehend how God could freely and unconditionally forgive me and take me back. It was inconceivable to think God would offer such unmerited grace and mercy without conditions. These spiritually gifted artists were leading me in a new way to praise our holy King while teaching me how to let go of my guilt and shame. This pattern of heavenly worship was where I continually surrendered myself and exalted my Redeemer. It was Jesus' wounds that were exchanged for the healing and restoring of mine.

By the time worship finished, my mind and spirit were poured out and ready to receive God's truth in His word. At first, I was perplexed because I was actually comprehending and enjoying the message the pastor was teaching. The Good News was no longer a feared message of condemnation and judgment, but of enlightenment and freedom. My soul was absorbing as much as it could, yet, I was hungry for more.

Every summer, Dave and Phuc's church held an annual baptism service at the Shawnee Mission Lake. This was Dave and Phuc's favorite time of the year because the church's ceremony was held outside at the lakeside amphitheater.

After the service, they all gathered at the edge of the lake for baptisms, followed by a picnic. I was dreading it. With such an open and large gathering, I would undoubtedly have to mingle with other people. Dave and Phuc promised me they would stay by my side, so I gave in and said I would go.

Sitting in the warmth of the sun's rays and feeling the breeze of the wind touch my face was a surreal moment. It felt like God was sitting right next to me. After the service ended, we slowly meandered, coolers and lawn chairs in hand, to the edge of the lake. They had already started the baptisms, and I could hear the sounds of crowds of people clapping and cheering as people rose out of the water. I was so relieved to think that the most immediate decision I had to make was choosing which tent to head to for shade.

I had to stand on my tiptoes to see over the wall of people. I was curious to see who was at the center of attention. With great enthusiasm, a few individuals stepped out of the crowd and publicly shared their testimonies and professed their everlasting faith in God. In one way or another, each person's testimony began to resonate with mine. Each story of redemption tugged at my spirit, pulling me in closer. I could feel the tears welling in my eyes, and my knees weakened. I wanted to step forward, but my body froze like a statue. I wanted to profess my love for God, but I was not ready to go public with my story. I still did not trust God's people. I had to immediately leave the tent, or the power of the moment would have swept me in.

As I quickly backpedaled, my mind began rationalizing my actions. I was baptized when I was thirteen years old, so it did not make any sense to do it again. Secondly, I was not ready to share my testimony in front of a large crowd of heterosexual Christians. Not to mention that I was petrified to speak in front of a large group. For God to ask me to openly share my testimony in front of strangers felt like a public crucifixion. I had no understanding of the real meaning of baptism, which was clear evidence that it was not my time.

Dave and Phuc later delivered some heartbreaking news. They were soon moving out of state. They were so excited about the move because it benefited their family, which made it hard for my daughter and I to feel disappointed. We celebrated our last day together with a meal and then they were gone. With never having healthy heterosexual friendships before, it was hard for me to know how to react. I was terrible at long-distance friendships, so I knew I would lose touch.

We continued attending Dave and Phuc's church for a while longer, but without them there, my daughter and I felt lost in the crowd. Neither of us made any new connections with others, and the church never felt like our church. I was once again searching for a church and on the lookout for another sign from God.

Shortly after starting kindergarten, my daughter made another new best friend. From the first day they met, they were inseparable. As before, I immediately connected and became close friends with the new friend's mother. Linda and her husband Bruce were Christians who generously invited us into their home and, eventually, to their church. I opened up and shared my story with them as well, and they too embraced and accepted me. Since I was on the hunt for another church, their invitation was perfectly timed, and I eagerly accepted.

They were regularly attending Westside Family Church on the western edge of Kansas City, Kansas. Although Westside was a megachurch with a congregation of over five thousand, we were still synergized and connected to these people. After our first visit to one of the three Sunday morning services, I instantly knew this was the place God wanted us to be. Between their gravitating, rock-solid children's ministry and the wooing of their spiritually-gifted pastors, my daughter and I were drawn to this church's atmosphere.

Nearly three years after surrendering my life to God, we had finally found our church family. Never in my life had I felt enthusiastic about going to church, and certainly not every Sunday. For the past three decades, I had either gone to a church when I desperately needed help from God or to temporarily rid myself of massive guilt. In both situations, it was self-serving. My motives were driven by my needs and had nothing to do with genuinely knowing and pleasing God. This time, church had a whole new meaning. The church was a family of believers sharing a place of fellowship, worship, and spiritual community. We all came together for one purpose—to know, obey, and share the love of God and His son Jesus. Westside Family Church's mission statement was spot on—loving Jesus, becoming like Jesus, and sharing Jesus.

Whenever I got settled and content in my spiritual walk, God would soon push me back out of my comfort zone. I was beginning to believe that the more uncomfortable and anxious I felt about my spiritual path, the more I knew it was God moving me out and the Holy Spirit moving in. The old had to leave before there was room for the new.

Meeting Jesus—Face to Face

Who are you, Lord? I asked.
I am Jesus of Nazareth, whom you are persecuting, he replied.
Jesus (Acts 22:8)

Just weeks after joining Westside Family Church, God used our friends to lead us to our next spiritual step. They wanted us to come and try out their small group. Besides not knowing the purpose of a life group, the thought of revealing my story to a group of strangers was more than enough reason to say no. I was starting to recognize the familiar patterns of the bombarding attacks from the enemy every time I was about to take a big leap in faith. Thankfully, it was God, not the tactics of the enemy, that motivated my obedience. Despite the paralyzing doubts and fears, I managed to say yes.

The small life group consisted of six heterosexual married couples led by Loren and Jen. From the moment I was introduced, I felt like the odd duck because I was not married. It helped having Bruce and Linda with me, but I initially struggled with relating to these people.

Besides not having a husband by my side or a track record of heterosexuality, I was more or less unchurched. When it came to open discussions on the Bible or what we thought it was saying to us, I had far more questions than comments. My daughter, on the other hand, had quite the opposite experience. She loved our group's weekly meetings because five out of the six families had young children around her age, including her best friend.

Although this group of people was amazingly funny, loving, and accepting, I was still fearful and reluctant to reveal my past and share my redemption story. I was already invested in this group, and their acceptance and approval mattered a lot to me. What I truly appreciated about this group of people was their respect for my privacy. Even after months of being together, no one pressured anyone into speaking or sharing. I took full advantage of their respectful generosity.

Then one afternoon, I got a call from our life group leader, Jen, asking me if I wanted to meet her for lunch. Although I said yes, I was a bit skeptical of her motives. Yet, the more I thought about it, the more it made sense. Every leader has the responsibility to reach out and press in with every group member. I welcomed her invitation, and I was prepared to share my story, but only if she asked.

We decided to meet in the middle of the week at the Red Snapper restaurant located only minutes from my workplace. As soon as we finished ordering our meals, the waitress grabbed our menus and walked away, leaving us sitting face to face. Jen was an extroverted champion at social conversations, so I waited for her lead. She quickly eased us into a bit of polite small talk. Then, before she could say another word, I teared up and blurted out, "I have something I need to tell you." Out of nervous jitters, I spieled off my testimony in a one-minute live podcast. After I finished, I anxiously waited for her response. Without a blink of an eye, she leaned in closer and softly said, "It is okay. I understand." To my amazement, she was already experienced in dealing with others struggling with taboo ways of life. I could finally exhale a sigh of relief.

After we exchanged details, I had to share my latest revelation. I followed up with saying, "I think I know how Jesus feels about homosexuality." I could tell that my comment caught her by surprise since it was coming from this shy and unchurched person who rarely talked about Jesus or herself.

I started into what happened to me a few months earlier. I had challenged God to show me in the Bible where it stated how He felt about homosexuality. I knew all six passages that most pastors, preachers, and Christians often referenced in regard to homosexual sin: Genesis 19:5, Leviticus 18:22 and 20:13, Romans 1:18-32, 1 Timothy 1:8-11, and 1 Corinthians 6:9-11. Personally, I could not identify my homosexual feelings or behavior with any of these verses. I also did not feel these verses accurately identified how God felt toward homosexuals. Instead, these verses pointed more toward the view of the behavior and categorized sin, not the heart motives that could be potentially driving the behavior. I was not questioning or doubting the sin aspect of the practice because I had already been convicted of it. I wanted to know what God thought about LGBTQ people in general. I made my prayer request and then went on with my business. Then God unexpectedly gave me a swift and incredible response that completely changed my heart.

It all began when two Jehovah's Witness missionaries came by my home and left behind their pamphlets along with this little book titled, "The Greatest Man Who Ever Lived". The book's cover showed an image of Jesus teaching people from a hillside next to an olive tree. I did not understand and necessarily agree with the Jehovah's Witness religion and doctrine, but I had to read this book. After all, this was the man God truly wanted me to get to know. The book had one hundred and thirty-three pages of stories about Jesus, and I could not wait to get started.

As I read through each story of Jesus, I cross-referenced every story's Scripture to my newly purchased NIV study Bible. Between reading the printed stories and the referenced Scriptures, I was soon engrossed and captivated by this eccentric character named Jesus.

I landed on the book of John, chapter eight. It was one of the few chapters in my Bible that did not have a labeled heading, so I had to read the entire chapter to see if the passages lined up with the story I was reading in the book.

> *The teachers of the law and the Pharisees brought in a woman caught in adultery. They made her stand before the group and said to Jesus, "Teacher, this woman was caught in the act of adultery. In the Law, Moses commanded us to stone such women. Now, what do you say?"*
>
> *They were using this question as a trap, to have a basis for accusing him. But Jesus bent down and started to write on the ground with his finger.*
>
> *When they kept on questioning him, he straightened up and said to them, "Let anyone of you who is without sin be the first to throw a stone at her."*
>
> *Again, he stooped down and wrote on the ground.*
>
> *At this, those who heard began to go away one at a time, the older ones first, until only Jesus remained, with the woman still standing there.*
>
> *Jesus straightened up and asked her, "Woman, where are they? Has no one condemned you? No one, sir," she said.*
>
> *Then neither do I condemn you," Jesus declared. "Go now and leave your life of sin." (John 8:1-11)*

As I finished reading this passage, I could feel the presence of Jesus in the middle of my living room. I, too, was an adulterous woman. I was so overwhelmed with His love and acceptance that I could hardly grasp a breath between the sobbing cries. I knew God had answered my earlier question about what He really thought about homosexuality. God responded by personally introducing me to His Son, Jesus—face to face.

There were three significant truths that I quickly embraced about Jesus, the world around us, and myself that sum up the entire Gospel of Jesus.

#1 - Casting the First Stone

When they kept on questioning him, he straightened up and said to
them,
"Let anyone of you who is without sin be the first to throw a stone at
her."
John 8:7

They each dropped their stones, one by one, starting with the oldest. These gripped stones represented the indwelling sins of self-righteousness, judgment, hypocrisy, and the sin of not loving one another. What Jesus showed me in this passage was how churches treated people like me while blinded by their own sin. This passage represents a hierarchy of sin developed by humans, with homosexuality being the highest, non-redeemable sin. Jesus clearly illustrates in John 8:7 that unless we are without sin, we have no authority to judge or condemn the sin of others. We have no right to cast the first stone...the second we pick up our "first" stone, we have committed the sin of hypocrisy. There was only one person in this story who had the authority to judge sin, and that was Jesus. Only in Jesus' righteousness am I gracefully presented before God as flawless and holy. In Jesus' eyes, I was no longer a marginalized outcast.

#2 – No Condemnation

Jesus straightened up and asked her, "Woman, where are they? Has
no one condemned you? No one, sir," she said.
"Then neither do I condemn you," Jesus declared.
John 8:10-11

This is where I totally lost it. Here was the Son of Man, who had full authority to sentence me to death due to my sin, according to the Mosaic Law (Leviticus 18:22). Yet, out of unfailing love, He chose to sacrifice His innocent life to save mine (Leviticus 20:13). After thirty years of labeling God as a gay-hater and heartless ruler who cast down condemnation for my sin, He had already prepared a rescue plan thousands of years ago to save me. This single act of Jesus' mercy, goodness, and kindness toward this sinful woman opened my eyes to the absolute truth and grace in Jesus Christ. "For the law was given through Moses; grace and truth came through Jesus Christ" (John 1:17). Jesus died in innocence for my guilty sin (truth), out of pure, untainted love (grace). This revelation branded my heart with the true meaning of the Gospel of Jesus.

#3 - Leave Your Life of Sin

Go now, and leave your life of sin.
John 8:11b

The undeniable truth was my homosexual way of life was a "life of sin" that God commanded me to leave. God did not condemn me for it. Instead, He gave me a way out through the victory of Jesus.

By Jesus conquering death on behalf of the world's imprisoning sin, I, undeservingly, was given everlasting freedom. There is *no* greater love than this.

Kingdom Identity

For those who are led by the Spirit of God are the children of God.
The Spirit you received does not make you slaves so that you live in
fear again;
rather, the Spirit you received brought about your adoption to
sonship.
And by him we cry, "Abba, Father."
Romans 8:14-15

It was through the revelatory truth unveiled in John 8:1-11 that I came to know Jesus. Not only did these verses teach me about the greatest Son of Man that ever lived, but that it was Jesus who set me free from the condemnation and captivity of my sin. I am a sister in the Body of Christ who no longer fears what other believers and nonbelievers think of me. I know how my Father feels about me, and that is enough. "The Spirit himself testifies with our spirit that we are God's children. Now if we are children, then we are heirs—heirs of God and coheirs with Christ if indeed we share in his sufferings so that we may also share in his glory" (Romans 8:16-17).

By the blood and body of Jesus Christ and the hands and feet of His many disciples who invited me in, this once-abandoned child was rescued, ransomed, and adopted into God's royal family.

From my heart and soul, I no longer questioned where I belonged. I can assuredly say I will forever reside in my Father's house, where He has prepared a place for me. I eternally belong to the Body of Jesus Christ, the Church.

I am a believer and follower of Jesus Christ. This was, and is, and will forever be my kingdom identity.

13

A DISCIPLE'S HEART

As you sent me into the world, I have sent them into the world.
Jesus (John 17:18)

Out of the Water

Westside Family Church started a new series of classes to help people find their next spiritual steps. After listening to my story, Jen recommended that I check them out. I registered for the first class called "Get Connected". The course was led by Westside's lead teaching pastors, Dan and Brian.

I fully surrendered my old self to God in June 2007, and three years later, I was finally prepared to be baptized. From the moment I made this monumental decision, I was compelled to tell my redemption story to whomever God put in front of me.

As to be expected, my boldness was immediately tested. When I submitted my request to be baptized, I had to write a brief description as to why I wanted to be baptized. Not only was I placing my homosexuality, gay identity, and intentional masculinity into a pinewood coffin box, I was nailing it airtight. I was not sealing my coffin because I was afraid of my past but rather out of victorious freedom. Through Jesus, my fight was over. I was fully confident in my answer.

My next step was opening up and telling everyone in my small group. God set the stage. In our group's next gathering, the topic of kingdom purpose and calling surfaced. We each took turns sharing what we thought our God-given purpose was and who might be the people God wanted us to serve. Then it was my turn, and I turned to Jen and said, "I guess it is time I tell everyone." I went on, "To tell what I think God wants me to do, I have to first tell my story." I gave about a two-minute testimony that felt like it went on for hours. After I finished, I shared that in some way, I felt that God was going to use my old life as well as my new life for His purpose. I just did not know when, what, where, or who.

Everyone was accepting, supportive, and excited to hear what God was doing in my life. What no one realized at the time was the fact that God was already at work in and through each person in this group, drawing me nearer to Jesus and His mission field. The wall that once separated this sexual-minority woman from her archenemy, heterosexual Christians, was coming down.

I was down to forty-eight hours before the celebratory day when I came down with a horrible virus. For twenty-four hours, I was sick with flu-like symptoms. Even though I was so discouraged and disappointed, I refused to give in. I immediately called the church office and rescheduled for the next baptismal Sunday, which was March 20, 2011.

On March 20th, I met my family, friends, and members of my small group in the front row of the sanctuary. The baptism tub was rolled out and filled with clear warm water. Just before the service started, Jen came and sat behind me and placed her hand on my shoulder. She smiled and calmly said, "Are you ready?" I replied with a big grin, "Yes, I am!" "Well, I know why God made you wait for today," she said. I whipped my body fully around, asking, "Seriously, you do?" She then said, "Just wait and listen to the message."

After worship finished, the pastor came out and introduced his message. His opening statement started with the passage from John 8:1-11, the account of Jesus and the adulterous woman. I could not believe what I was hearing. God chose to anoint my resurrection day with the same Scripture that introduced me to Jesus. To put the icing on the cake, our pastors were teaching a four-week message series called "Sent". This was the summary of the series:

- I am a priest

- Jesus has called me into ministry

- Jesus has gifted and equipped me for ministry

- Jesus has given me a group of people to serve
- I will answer His call

Once I came out of the water like Jesus, I was called to be a priestly disciple to a chosen group of people. However, I did not know what it meant to be called and equipped for ministry. All I knew was that I had a whole lot of love and passion for the LGBTQ community. I wanted them to meet the Jesus that I had met. If passion was the primary indicator of a given calling, then I was ready to answer His call with a definite yes. I was all in but had no clue how to get started.

Our Character and Calling

I am confident that God, who began the good work within you, will continue his work until it is finally finished on the day when Christ Jesus returns.
Philippians 1:6

Like every zealous convert, I was on fire to serve even though I was not equipped or given a clear mission. A missionary that goes into the mission field without first knowing God's plan is a foolish one. In the beginning of my spiritual walk, that described me.

As a seasoned leader, Jen recognized my awakened passion and wanted to get me connected to the right people. She put me in contact with Westside's pastor, Brian, the same pastor that co-led my Get Connected class.

On a Sunday morning, after one of Westside's services, Jen and I met with Brian. I was so nervous to speak with Brian because he was a pastor and I had no idea how he would react to me or my story. After a brief introduction, Brian asked if I would be willing to share a little about myself. As I sat on the couch next to Jen in Brian's small office, I started to tell my story from the beginning to where I was currently in my spiritual journey. At one point in the conversation, I outwardly stated that if Christians would open their doors to the LGBTQ people and get out of God's way, more people like me would find Jesus. I was a bit shocked at the things that were rolling out of my mouth.

Once I had finished talking, Brian's words were affirming. He smiled and calmly said something like, "That is an amazing story. God is going to use you, Karol, and I can't wait to see how He does it." I really had no understanding of what he was talking about and what he meant by God using me. All I was thinking about was finishing the conversation as quickly as I could.

God would soon use my conversation with Pastor Brian for His purpose. Brian had recently launched his non-profit organization called "Disciples Made". Disciples Made is a suite of disciple-making experiences designed to bring transformation to our local faith communities by training and equipping people to become missionaries where they live, work, learn, and play.

A few months after our conversation, Brian circled back to me and presented an opportunity to join in the first series of Disciples Made experience called Followers Made. Followers Made is a transformative, six-month experience that helps participants develop Jesus-like character and begin to discover their unique calling. Without hesitation, I jumped in with both feet. I was more focused on increasing my spiritual growth than my concern over my lack of it.

By Brian's instruction, I reached out and contacted his appointed leader of an upcoming women's Followers Made group, Breanna, or Bre for short. When I told her that I wanted to sign up for her Followers Made group, she was more than thrilled to assign me a spot. After welcoming me, she informed me of the start date in January 2013, which was only four months away.

As Bre and I got to know each other over the next few months, she shared with me her Followers Made (FM) group line-up. Eleven women were joining her FM group, making it a total of twelve women. As Bre went down the list of names, I could feel my heart pounding as I went into panic mode. I was out of my league and, not to mention, I was once a lesbian. I felt as though I was the least of the least and unqualified.

Bre then threw out another grenade. She said, "Karol, God has put a light bulb over your head as a potential co-leader." I was speechless. Then after the sting let up, I said, "Why would God choose me? Bre, I need to tell you something. In my past, I lived as a homosexual. I am no longer same-sex-attracted, but these women do not know that. I do not know how to relate to heterosexual Christian women. Bre, are you sure?" She was confident in what God was showing her. Then I fearfully replied, "Who am I to question God? If God has spoken to you, then I have to obey." That became my new spiritual mantra. I was not educating God on anything that He already did not know.

We had our first gathering at a small café in Price Chopper. Bre kicked off the meeting by asking us to briefly share where we were serving in the kingdom. I was like, well, here we go again. Then she turned and nodded for me to go. Both of my feet were bouncing off the floor as I tried to release all my nervous energy. I shared the highlights of my story and explained why I was in this group. One woman started to cry. She went next and quickly explained why my story touched her. She shared, "I have been praying for God to find me a group of real women who wanted to pursue a real God. I know why I am here." On the first night, there was a special spiritual connection between all the women. Every woman was excited and willing to hear more about my testimony, and they embraced and accepted me from the moment we met. Well, almost every woman.

During our second meeting, Laura, who missed our first gathering, arrived a few minutes late. The only empty seat left around our small table was next to me. Immediately, I sensed that this woman did *not* like me. By the end of the meeting, her actions toward me remained hardened. I, on the other hand, enjoyed Laura. She was funny and spirited. I instinctively knew that whatever was bothering her had nothing to do with me, and I was okay with the situation.

Laura caught a ride home that night with Michelle, her close friend, and the truth came out. "There is something fishy here about our co-leader, Karol. I know she is a lesbian." Michelle smiled and chuckled a bit. Then she said, "Well, funny you would say that. As a matter of fact, she told us on the first night that she used to be a lesbian until she met Jesus. That is her redemption story." Laura did not buy into it. Her thoughts were, once gay, always gay. No one just walks away from homosexuality.

As weeks passed, Laura kept her distance from me. After spending five months together, meeting weekly, Laura finally had a breakthrough. I discovered the subject of homosexuality was extremely personal and painful for her. She had lost her older brother to AIDS after he had lived as a homosexual for many years. Because of the tragic loss of her beloved brother, Laura deeply resented all aspects of homosexuality, me included.

As Laura opened up and shared her story, God began to restore and reconcile two sisters in Christ to His truth—His love changes everything, even a LGBTQ person.

When it came to my Christ-like character, I discovered that my fleshly nature had layers of sin that I needed to peel back like an onion. Once I peeled back an outer layer, I would then expose a deeper layer of rooted sin. Everyone presumed all of my sins were based on my sexual immorality, but what people overlooked and disregarded were my covert sins like greed, pride, materialism, gossip, slander, and so on. I have often said that my sexual sin was merely the low-hanging fruit that the Spirit plucked first. Some people believed that it was just my sexual immorality that would have cast me into eternal hell. That was not the truth. What would have left me standing on the edge of eternal death was my disbelief that I was a sinner in need of Jesus and His forgiveness and righteousness. My only way back to God was through my faith in Jesus as my Savior.

As we neared the end of our twenty-four weeks of Followers Made, I had a breakthrough with my calling. God took me back to a year earlier, when I was asked to facilitate a break-out session on the topic of homosexuality at a Christian women's conference. What came as a surprise to me during that conference was that nearly all of the women who participated in my three repeated sessions were heterosexual women. It was the heterosexual Christians who were struggling the most with how to face the issues of homosexuality. That was whom God was calling me to help and serve.

Once I shared this discovery with my FM group, each woman not only confirmed it but confessed it. They too struggled with how they were to love and serve the LGBTQ community. With their unwavering support, I launched a new support group called Heart for the Homosexual. Its objective was to help others develop a Christlike heart and spirit toward His beloved LGBTQ people without having to sacrifice their conviction.

Over the past six years, I have learned that there are two sides to every LGBTQ person's story: theirs and their loved ones. I can fully testify that Jesus cares deeply about both sides. God is rebuilding the bridge and restoring His love between His people, from cisgender to queer and everything in between.

After just six months' engagement in Followers Made, I had learned how to become more like Jesus in character and locate my calling through my gifts, passions, and story. However, that was not all. Nine out of the eleven women chose to engage in another twelve months of Leaders Made. Bre and I willingly continued leading this experience that took us much wider and deeper into God's word and the doctrine of Christianity. It was in those twelve months that I discovered my passion and love for God's word. His word truly became my daily bread.

After experiencing such a deep, spiritual connection with these remarkabl women, they gave me confidence in the ability to develop and sustain healthy boundaries and loving relationships with other women. These women helped me identify myself as a woman of God and as the person God had always meant for me to be. That was another miracle in my life.

These women modeled Jesus' true discipleship: we loved and supported each other wholeheartedly regardless of our imperfections. How purposeful it is when God's family all live as one, in perfect unity (Psalm 133:1).

A Disciple's Identity

><

Come, follow me, Jesus said, and I will send you out to fish for
people.
Jesus (Matthew 4:19)

I love to fish. I am not necessarily picky about the kind of fish I catch; I just love the thrill of seeing the bobber slightly dip below the surface of the water and feeling the wiggle and light tug on the fishing line. I can hardly wait to see, with my own eyes, the size, weight, and look of the fish I am about to reel in.

Even though I had read Matthew 4:19 numerous times, I was still missing Jesus' point about fishermen. That was, until God revealed to me in dream a different kind of fishing that forever changed my heart.

It was a remarkable sight. I had never seen so many species of fish in one aquarium before. The tank nearly consumed the entire floor space of this 10,000+ square feet building covered with high-rafted ceilings adjoined to ocean blue walls. It reminded me of an aquatic exhibit in places like SeaWorld.

I was awestruck by the different shapes, sizes, and hues of each fish. No two fish were alike. It was such a tranquil scene, watching the brilliantly colored fish swim effortlessly and gracefully through the clear water.

Suddenly, the aquarium was losing water—and fast! Within seconds, the water dropped halfway down from the top of the tank. As the water level continued to fall, the shocked fish began to surface, piling on top of each other. In a matter of minutes, there was a heap of dying fish stacked high above the water's surface. I watched in horror as their gills flared wide as they gasped for life. Their desperate attempts to thrust their dying bodies back into the water was futile.

Even if I was only able to save one fish, I had to act. I grabbed a large hose lying on the floor next to the aquarium. I followed the hose back to its water source and turned on the hydrant to full blast. As the water level began to slowly increase, a multitude of fish bubbled up to the surface. Their lifeless bodies stretched across the entire surface of the water and measured several feet deep. My heart sank as I realized how many fish were dying right before my eyes.

Leaning over the top of the tank, I frantically searched for signs of life. I repeatedly dipped my hands into the water, swirling through the stillness of dying fish. When I saw a glimmer of life, I gently scooped its body into my hands. I slowly submerged the dying fish into the water, hoping the flow of water would restore life. As the numbers of dead fish increased, I felt a sick feeling in my stomach. The substantial death was inconceivable.

I woke up from the dream with this disturbing imagery that left me with feelings of urgency, desperation, and loss.

Immediately, I started thinking about the meaning and symbolism of fish in the Bible, which motivated me to look up all the biblical references of fish. As my eyes landed on the word "fish", my heart sank with its meaning:

Fish = Souls of People

Staring down at three simple words, "souls of people," I could see the heart of God.

Here were my three takeaways from this vivid dream:

#1 – Fish Represent God's Creation

Every single fish symbolizes one living soul that God created "…in His own image" (Genesis 1:27a). The variety of sizes, shapes, and magnificent colors of fish testifies to God's diverse tapestry of mankind. Just like God's miraculous and beautiful rainbow, His covenant covers all humanity of the world, not just a single diverse group of people. The spectacular rainbow phenomenon is a glorious, living reminder of God's promise to never again destroy the earth and all inhabitants by a flood. As faithful disciples, we cannot discriminate against one kind of fish; we are to fish for all. Every diverse, living soul is never out of God's sight and Jesus' reach. His rainbow arches over all of mankind.

#2 – Running Out of Time

The rapidly falling water level represents the sense of urgency and the race against earthly time. Across the world, 6,316 people die each hour. Just like the piling up of fish, every day and every hour, God witnesses the death of many souls, and His heart mourns. Every person we meet is an opportunity to share the saving love of Jesus. As missionaries, we have to make every second and every encounter count.

#3 – Everlasting Life

"Whoever believes in me, as Scripture has said, rivers of living water will flow from within them." Those were the words spoken by Jesus to the woman at the well in John 7:38.

There is only one source that quenches all thirst and gives abundant life, and that is given through the righteous life of the most excellent fisherman, Jesus Christ.

A New Symbol of Identity

In the first few centuries of the early Church, Christians embraced the symbolism of the fish as their faith identity in Jesus Christ. Because of the ongoing persecution toward early Christians, the fish symbol served as a way for the early Christians to secretly identify other believers who were born-again followers of Jesus. They often left the mark of the fish symbol at their meeting places to distinguish friends from enemies. The emblem ⋗⋖ was universally known as the "Jesus fish". Being a "Jesus Fish" means being a disciple. Being a disciple means following Jesus with the same heart, mind, body, and spirit as His, and obeying whatever, whenever, and wherever He tells us. Listen to the mother of Jesus: "His mother said to the servants, 'Do whatever he tells you'" (John 2:5). It is a simple directive, yet hard to engage.

Fishing for people is the inevitable heart and identity of a true disciple of Jesus. I still enjoy catching fish, but nothing compares to my newfound passion for soul fishing. It is that supernatural passion that clearly identifies me as a disciple of Jesus.

14

RESURRECTED LOVE

A new command I give you: Love one another. As I have loved you,
so you must love one another. By this everyone will know
that you are my disciples if you love one another.
John 13:34-35

Love Multiplies

His resurrected love multiplies.

The first seed that God used to draw me back to Him was the one closest to my heart—my beloved daughter. Out of God's amazing love for my daughter and me, her tiny seed began to grow on its own.

Three months after my baptism, my daughter accepted Jesus as her Savior while participating in the Westside Family Church's Vacation Bible School program. At age seven, my daughter asked Jesus into her heart on July 31, 2011. Like it says in Mark 4:26-29 (NLT), "The Kingdom of God is like a farmer who scatters seed on the ground. Night and day, while he's asleep or awake, the seed sprouts and grows, but he does not understand how it happens. The earth produces the crops on its own. First, a leaf blade pushes through, then the heads of wheat are formed, and finally, the grain ripens. As soon as the grain is ready, the farmer comes and harvests it with a sickle, for the harvest time has come." I am an eyewitness to Jesus' love multiplying in my life and the lives placed around me.

As I continued serving families through the Heart for the Homosexual groups, I witnessed people reconnecting with their LGBTQ loved ones by discovering how to love one another without losing their convictions. Here are just some of those stories.

Andy and Luanna, based on the love of Jesus, were the first parents to radically change their hearts toward their gay son. After years of having close fellowship with the members of their hometown church, they were feeling compelled to leave their once close-knit congregation based on one simple truth—Jesus loves everyone. Once the church leaders had learned that one of Andy and Luanna's sons was gay, they unanimously ruled to segregate their gay son from the church. Andy and Luanna found themselves shunned and isolated from a congregation they once trusted. They were at a crossroad. They either had to follow Jesus, who they believed loved all people, or support the people who had ultimately rejected them and their son. Love had to come first.

After months of heartfelt prayers and deliberation, Andy and Luanna left their church and rooted themselves in Westside Family Church. Their ongoing desire was to see churches move toward greater inclusion of LGBTQ men and women. Inclusion does not mean we approve of sin, but rather obey the commandment to love others as Jesus loves us. Andy and Luanna chose to walk in truth and grace.

Then there were my friends Les and Michelle, whom I met through my first church life group led by Jen and Loren. Les and Michelle were facing a life crisis after their adult son told them he was gay. After raising their son for twenty-three years, they had no idea he had been wrestling with his sexual identity. They felt betrayed as well as heartbroken. I offered them two promising propositions.

First and foremost, I encouraged them not to lose hope in God's resurrection power and redemption plan. Les and Michelle had witnessed what Jesus had done in my life, so they knew anything was possible. I also recommended they sign up for my next Heart for the Homosexual session, which they did.

It was in this next Heart for the Homosexual group that I saw the love of Jesus spread like a wildfire. Les and Michelle soon joined Westside Family Church and, not long after, they were baptized. They began pursuing their heart's passion and calling by leading a support group for parents with gay children called Healing Hearts. Jesus was extending his love to reach out to his latest disciples among his

LGBTQ children and their parents. Jesus' love was healing all kinds of family wounds and reconciling hearts.

Then there was Phil. I first met Phil through a pastor's referral. Phil had become close friends with his lesbian neighbors, who had two young sons together. He invested himself as a role model for the two boys by taking them fishing, hiking, and playing catch. This relationship soon put him in a unique situation that brought spiritual tension. The lesbian couple asked Phil to be their witness to their same-sex marriage at the courthouse. Now Phil's conviction was being challenged.

What gave Phil peace was when he felt God had given him permission to stand firm in his faith and trust the work of the Holy Spirit. I told Phil that his relationship with these women was the outcome of the Holy Spirit's work in and through Phil. If God had indeed brought these women into his life, and if Phil trusted God, God would finish what He had started.

Phil declined the women's invitation to witness, not out of rejection or judgment, but out of his faith and conviction. These women respected Phil's decision even though they did not agree with it. They had accepted Phil as he had received and accepted them. Even in our differences, we can ask for mutual respect.

After his breakthrough with his lesbian neighbors, Phil and his wife Sheila soon joined one of my Heart for the Homosexual groups. It just so happened that Phil's younger brother was also gay and had been married to his same-sex partner for five years. Phil had spent years struggling with how to love his brother despite his homophobia and condemnation. Phil now felt affirmed in how to love his brother as well as his lesbian neighbors and not lose his faith or conviction. Phil says it well: "After all, we are all dealing with issues of the heart."

Phil realized his passion and calling. Because of his newfound love for the hurting and forsaken, Phil decided to join Westside's Stephen Ministry team. Trained Stephen Ministers provide one-on-one confidential care between the caregiver (Stephen Minister) and the care-receiver. Not long after Phil began his journey with Stephen Ministry, Sheila, and Phil's sister, Lori, also became Stephen Ministers.

Over the past seven years, I have seen the love of Jesus continue to multiply among his chosen disciples in the most unexpected ways.

Love Frees

His resurrected love frees us.

In addition to ministering to families and friends with LGBTQ loved ones, I found myself walking alongside other Christians within the Body of Christ. Whether speaking at conferences or in private settings, my purpose was and is to always bring truth and hope in Jesus' resurrected love to often messy and difficult conversations concerning homosexuality and transgender issues. "Then you will know the truth, and the truth will set you free" (John 8:32).

My friend Erin found the freedom to love others while remaining grounded in her faith. Here is her story in her words.

I first met Karol at a gathering of speakers for a women's conference intended to help women from around the country find wholeness in Christ. Each leader had a different testimony of redeemed brokenness that gave other women hope. I plainly remember seeing Karol sitting directly across from me as we circled up to pray and share our testimony and the message God had given us each to share. I knew many of the women in that room. Friends and colleagues who had lived redeemed lives vulnerably shared their brokenness and God's goodness in His restoration of their hearts and lives. I did not know Karol, yet I somehow instinctively knew she was there to share regarding homosexuality—and I just couldn't go there. There only seemed to be two sides to this issue when it came to the topic of homosexuality in the church. When it was talked about, I could not get on board with either side. Having grown up in Topeka, Kansas—home to Fred Phelps and the Westboro Church—and with a gay family member I deeply loved, I was not okay with the gay-bashing. I was also not okay with the church's affirmation of any sexual immorality—mine or someone same-sex-attracted. In my experience, there just was nothing in between, so like many churches, it was more comfortable to just back up from the topic altogether.

That afternoon, as we went around the circle sharing, I became increasingly more uncomfortable as we got closer to Karol's turn to share. What would she say? How would I respond? And then, finally, it was Karol's turn. From the minute she opened her mouth and began to share, everyone leaned in. Her story of grace and redemption, of restoration and wholeness, and her heart for the LGBTQ...she perfectly articulated the power of the living God moving and active in her heart and life in such a way that we all could relate and celebrate. She was *for* people who were transgender, same-sex-attracted, or living as gay-identified. And she was *for* God—His grace and truth and the power of the word living in us. Karol shared her testimony and, although I had never been same-sex-attracted, her story was my story. Lost and then found—a resurrected heart and changed life—and someone who now wanted others to experience the same freedom in Christ that she had seen. For both those who were same-sex-attracted and those who loved them.

Karol's story and testimony helped me experience a new level of redemption that continues to allow me to walk in freedom. Freedom that enables me to love all people freely, without question. For all people were created in the image of God and deeply, eternally loved by our Heavenly Father. The Karols and the Erins of the world. Karol has taught me what Christ has been speaking forth from his word for generations. We are called to do two things, the greatest of commandments: Love God. Love people.

Love Heals

His resurrected love heals us.

There was one particular story that forever changed lives, including my own. It is my friend Eden's story. The name Eden means "delight", which is the name God gave his garden. Everyone who had encountered Eden somehow knew she was truly one of God's chosen.

I met Eden when she showed up unannounced to one of my Heart for the Homosexual groups. I kicked off the introduction by asking each person to take a few minutes to write down what they wanted to get out of the group. After a couple of minutes passed by, I started with the first person to my right, asking them to share with the group what they had written. One by one, each person expressed their concerns and challenges with connecting, loving, and accepting LGBTQ people. Eden was the last person to share.

The first words out of her mouth were that she was not sure she was in the right place after hearing everyone's thoughts and feelings on the issues of homosexuality.

As she started to tell us her story, tears streamed down her face. The doctors had diagnosed her with terminal cancer, but that was only half of the story. She told us she was in love with another woman and they had been happy together for the past ten years. Right after Eden learned she had cancer, her life partner abandoned her…for another woman. Eden's heart was far more broken from the abandonment and betrayal of her partner than the terminal prognosis of her cancer.

After Eden finished sharing and settled down emotionally, the room was silent. Her story had left us all speechless. Then every person, including Eden, turned to me, waiting for some lightning bolt of wisdom to come out of my mouth. I, too, was waiting for the same thing. I had no idea how to integrate an audience of one same-sex person and a group of heterosexual Christians. I was desperately praying for God to help me, and He did.

As Eden sat straight across the table from me, I felt like I was looking at myself, only seven years prior. Her cry for help took me back to the night where I too pleaded for God's help. It was at that moment that I knew what I needed to say. I assured Eden, with all the confidence from the heavens above, that she was right where God wanted her to be.

I nervously began teaching from my redemption story: the how, when, and why I started down the path of homosexuality and how God turned everything around. After giving my closing statement, I immediately opened the floor for questions and discussions. Eden again began to pour out her soul. One woman in the group was a youth leader at Westside who was spiritually gifted with intercessory prayer. She spoke up and said, "I believe we need to pray for Eden."

Immediately, the atmosphere of the room shifted. Every person got up from their chairs and circled Eden, and, one by one, we all began to pray. It was like time stood still. Here was a room full of heterosexual Christians, male and female, who came to learn how to love the LGBTQ community, and, before the hour had passed, Jesus was fulfilling their heart's desires. Through Eden, Jesus taught all of us, gay or straight, to love without hesitation, to have humility for the hurting, to unite with compassion, and have hope in transformation.

Our journey with Eden continued for a little while longer. We all knew Eden's earthly story was near its end, but her heavenly story would soon begin. During one of my last visits with Eden, I told her I could not stay long because I had a one-on-one meeting with a young gentleman who was also wrestling with his gender and sexual identity. She looked me directly in the eyes and said, "Karol, be sure and tell him how much God loves him. It is all about God's love." Miraculously, Eden's heart was turned by the love of Jesus. In some solitary moment between Eden and God, she repented of her life and gave her heart to Jesus. As one of her many eyewitnesses, I watched Eden change from a self-doubting person who was fearful of eternal salvation to a beloved child of God.

The last time I spoke with Eden was just days before she passed away. As I sat alone by her side, I leaned over and whispered in her ear, "Eden, it is Karol." She quickly opened her eyes and said, "Karol? Am I in heaven?" As I pushed back the tears and cleared the lump out of my throat, I replied, "No, not yet."

My last words to Eden were unusual, yet accurate. "Eden, I will see you soon." I felt compelled to say this because I knew it was not a lasting goodbye. It will only be a short time before I will see Eden's radiant blue eyes and delightful smile again as I see her standing by our shared love—Jesus.

Love Cultivates

His resurrected love cultivates us.

These impact stories inspired me to keep leaning in and pushing Jesus' love forward. In the summer of 2015, I established a 501c3 ministry called SOIL (Step Out In Love) Ministries. SOIL's mission is to cultivate the love of Jesus into the hearts of his LGBTQ people from either side. The ministry of SOIL is founded in the parable Jesus shared in Matthew 13:1-23, about the sown seed and the different kinds of soil. Each soil represented the conditions of people's hearts: some were hearts deceived, some were rock hard, and some choked from the truth. However, it only takes one tiny seed to grow in fertile soil to yield a hundred times itself. It is God's written promises like these that kept me digging deeper.

In 2017, God opened a door directly to the LGBTQ community. I was ready to serve, but again, I did not know how, who, or when. I had to wait. Eventually, God took me right back to the person who helped me take my first ministry step, Pastor Brian. I shared my vision and burden, and I was delightfully surprised to find out that God had already placed a similar passion for the LGBTQ community on Brian's heart.

Brian had recently developed an IDE model, Intentional Disciple-Making Environments, where leaders tailor their disciple-making framework toward their God-given purpose, people, and mission. A pathway was shown. Together, we developed a disciple-making pilot called Identity Made. The mission of Identity Made was to help sexual minority people integrate their faith in Jesus and their alternative sexuality into the Body of Christ and find confidence in their resurrected identity. My journey from an exiled foreigner to a united believer was no easy feat. It was not a path God intended for anyone to walk alone.

Sexual immorality was not a new sin for the church. Heterosexual Christians often struggle with adultery, pornography, sexual addiction, and so on. The church was willingly and readily available to support this kind of sexual immorality. Nevertheless, for some unknown reason, when it came to the struggles of the LGBTQ community, the church often avoided their needs and left them feeling hopeless and helpless. There was, and still is, a great need for Identity Made groups.

It was not long before my God-given co-leader, Kathi, and I launched our first Identity Made group. Kathi, a heterosexual wife and mother of seven children, had a heart for the forsaken. She served women in the strip club industry. Kathi and I were thrilled to have five women join our Identity Made group. Three of the IM women lived in three different states with three different time zones. For those living out of state, we included them through live Zoom video sessions every week.

After sharing a twenty-four-week journey, the six of us celebrated with a three-day retreat in the heart of Kansas City. Besides all of the shared home-cooked meals and fun outings, our grand finale was celebrating a baptism. Sophie, who was my closest friend during the period I was with Jamie, committed her life to Jesus. However, where we had planned to have the baptism was changed at the last minute. We ended up baptizing Sophie in Westside Family Church's lake during the middle of February. It was a glorious moment, even though the water was freezing!

There were many crucial, life-changing outcomes from Identity Made. Initially, each woman found themselves either disconnected or alienated from the church for one reason or another. Some women struggled with past hurt and trauma inflicted by other Christians, while others feared what Christians would think if they knew they were same-sex-attracted. Lastly, some were intimidated by Christianity as a whole. Every woman, at some level, feared rejection by the Christian community.

Their sexuality was just one aspect of their challenges that kept them from growing spiritually. All these stumbling blocks were keeping these women bound to an incomplete identity in Jesus. The saddest fact was that none of these women felt they could be transparent with their 'as is' lives in the Christian community. That was at the core of every woman's heart issue.

Identity Made is not some reparative program intended to covertly or inadvertently change anyone's sexual attractions, sexual orientation, or sexual identity. The mission of Identity Made is to help people like me with similar gender or sexual backgrounds live in the unfathomable depth of Jesus' love and grow into the character and identity of Jesus Christ. Eternal salvation and transformation are not just a gift from God; it is a *gift of God*, given only through the sprinkling of Jesus' blood. LGBTQ people can inherit this gift, too.

Love Unites

His resurrected love unites us.

One of the most valuable lessons I have learned about Jesus is that He is always with us and unites us with the right people at the right time and for every purpose. Whether we need friendships, spiritual accountability and mentoring, or leadership, God will provide and unite us, time and time again, with the right resources at the perfect time. It is in and through these relationships with others that we can truly experience the transformational power of Jesus' love in ourselves and others.

My Identity Made co-leader, Kathi, is just one example in how God linked us together for our personal needs as well as His purpose. Kathi testifies to this.

I wholeheartedly believe that when God puts people into our lives, He gives us the kind of people He knows we need. When Karol came into my life over eight years ago, she had a bigger-than-life story that she was still trying to reconcile through. What I didn't know at the time is that I had a front row seat to seeing God work in her and through her, all while she was battling her own insecurities and plowing through the lies that the enemy was trying to feed her. I admire Karol for not letting fear keep her from what God set forth in her heart.

Karol and I have journeyed along through our individual ministry work and then God aligned us to partner together through the work of Identity Made. I cherish her as one of my closest friends, and our families are close, too. Karol is the kind of friend who was mentioned in Mark 2—when Jesus was speaking to a group of people and some men couldn't get their friend in the door, they lowered their friend in from the roof, so the man could sit at Jesus' feet. We all need friends like this—ones who will go to great lengths when we cannot do it on our own. Over the years, I've seen Karol have faith in families that did not have faith of their own. She serves tirelessly until it hurts. What a true honor to carry out Jesus' mission alongside her and learn from her.

Some scoffers will criticize the work she is doing. When we are criticized for loving "the wrong people", that just means we are doing something right. This is how Jesus lived and modeled life, and I'm so grateful for this example in my life!

Love Identity

If I have a faith that can move mountains but do not have love, I am nothing.
If I give all I possess to the poor and give over my body to hardship that I may boast, but do not have love, I gain nothing.
1 Corinthians 13:2-3

It is Jesus' resurrected love that fully identifies His disciples.

The most profound truth that God has taught me through my redemption story is this: Jesus' resurrected love is the transformational power that changes us from the inside out, regardless of our past lives. "…A person who has no love is still dead" (1 John 3:14b NLT). The most significant evidence of a true disciple is how they love others.

If we fail to love others the way Jesus loves us, with shared humility, unity, and hope, then we have failed at *everything*!

15

I AM

I am who I am.
Jesus (John 13:19)

His Given Name

The most significant statement a person can make is *I am*. What we use to fill in our *I am* statement is highly significant to our identity, but most importantly, to our spiritual lives. It is how we want to be known by others.

It was God who created the *I am* statement. He first declared himself as "I AM" to identify His supreme authority, power, and omnipresence among His chosen Israelites. God declared Himself to Moses in Exodus 3:14 as, "I AM WHO I AM". He directs Moses, "This is what you are to say to the Israelites: 'I AM has sent me to you.'" It is the name by which God made known to all His Jewish people, and, later, to all Gentiles. The name I AM is how God expresses and identifies his character as the dependable, good, and faithful God who desires the full trust of His people. When God speaks of himself, he says, "I AM", and when we talk of Him and worship Him, we say, "He is."

Jesus applies I AM to himself, identifying Himself as the Son of God. In a defining moment, Jesus asked Peter, "Who do you say I am?" Peter captured Jesus' name and identity in his reply by declaring Jesus as "God's Messiah" (Luke 9:20). Jesus reiterates

145

his given name in John 8:58, "'Very truly I tell you,' Jesus answered, 'before Abraham was born, I am!'" Then, in John 13:19, He says, "I am telling you now before it happens so that when it does happen, you will believe that I AM WHO I AM."

It is the *I am* statement that reflects the most significant worth and highest value we place on our identity. What we put behind *I am* in terms of our spiritual identity is the most indicative of our salvation. Jesus tells us how we should identify ourselves in Luke 12:8: "I tell you, whoever publicly acknowledges me before others, the Son of Man will also acknowledge before the angels of God." Our lives should be a public acknowledgement of His name and identity. Nothing more and nothing less.

I have no doubt that my salvation was at risk before saying yes to God in June 2007. All the evidence was bundled in my self-made identity. For three decades, I proudly proclaimed my self-defined identity with a declaration statement of—*I am gay*. With that given name, I was known only by the gods I worshipped, not Jesus. Like the false prophets of Baal in 1 Kings 18, their altar remained unlit while the one true God, through the real prophet of Elijah, lit the altar, and everything around it burned to the ground with purifying fire. When I finally woke up from years of deception, I found myself kneeling at a cold, wet, and dark altar. I realized that my idolized gods could never deliver me.

At the beginning of this story, I shared that my given name, Karol, means "a song of joy". I believe my name has fulfilled its spiritual purpose because my joy is now complete in the name and identity of Jesus (John 3:29). Notably, my daughter's earthly name is Emma, and it means "complete". Through God's sovereignty and grace, He chose to complete my life through the *given* life of my daughter Emma. To God, our names have a divine purpose.

His Resurrected Identity

I have been crucified with Christ and I no longer live, but Christ lives in me.
Galatians 2:20

Crucified and buried.

There is no other way into the Kingdom of Heaven other than choosing to crucify and bury our old lives along with Jesus Christ through the repentance of our sin. Everything about me and my self-made identity had to die and be buried. There were no compromises.

The last part of my identity that I refused to surrender to God was the first to be sacrificed on the holy altar—my homosexuality and gay identity. These two were the gods that I continued to worship. Our God is a jealous God and He will not stand for other idols before Him.

If we have truly crucified ourselves, then we have put all sins, including those that once owned us, and all of our idols to death. To receive the resurrected identity of Jesus, we have to identify our penitent lives with His death. Death to sin is the only way to inherit life.

For we died and were buried with Christ by baptism.
And just as Christ was raised from the dead by the glorious power of
the Father,
now we also may live new lives. Since we have been united with him
in his death,
we will also be raised to life as he was.
Romans 6:4-5 (NLT)

Resurrected.

Since we have been identified with Jesus in his death, we are surely identified with Him through a resurrected life. The same resurrection power that raised Jesus also raised us (Romans 8:11). That is when everything inside of us changes. Our minds are renewed, our sins are defeated, and our hearts are resurrected in love. I still have the same face, body, and quirky sense of humor, but my character, heart, and spirit have radically transformed. I am now second and Jesus is first.

The greatest proof of my life's transformation came out of the mouth of my mother. Not long ago, she shook her head in amazement and said, "Karol, something about you has changed. You are anchored like a rock." I went from the identity of a "freak" to an "anchored rock", and not by my own doing. My mother is just one eyewitness to the power of the Holy Spirit living within me.

Christians are to be living witnesses to the resurrection of the living Jesus. The evidence is in our resurrected identity that is built on the foundation of God's redemption. A resurrected identity radiates from a disciple's awakened, chosen, reborn, adopted, discipled, and resurrected heart that is endlessly bound by the love of Jesus.

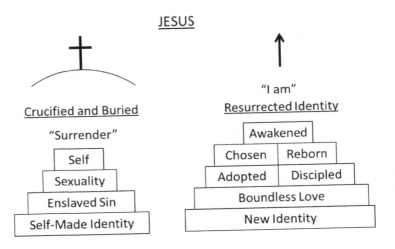

Personally, this image depicts the true identity of a Christian who is a genuine disciple of Jesus: from crucified and buried to resurrected by the power of God.

Coming out with Christ should be the declaration of every believer who identifies themselves with the crucifixion, death, and resurrection of the one true Messiah, Jesus Christ, (Romans 10:9). We all share in this statement: *"I am resurrected with Jesus Christ."*

Now is the time, a time such as this, for the Kingdom to come…to come out of our graves and declare who we truly are in Jesus Christ.

Made in the USA
Middletown, DE
29 August 2020